Love & Prejudice

Love & Prejudice

Unlearning Anti-Blackness as a South Asian

Sandeep Kaur

NEW DEGREE PRESS
COPYRIGHT © 2023 SANDEEP KAUR
All rights reserved.

LOVE & PREJUDICE
Unlearning Anti-Blackness as a South Asian

ISBN   979-8-88504-455-4 *Paperback*
           979-8-88926-633-4 *Hardcover*
           979-8-88504-479-0 *Ebook*

To Ishaani.
You are my compass.

Contents

Preface · 1

Introduction · 3

Part 1

CHAPTER 1. Growing Up a Brown Girl in a White World · 9

CHAPTER 2. The Roots of My Prejudice · 21

CHAPTER 3. A Blue-Eyed Boy and *The Vagina Monologues* · 33

CHAPTER 4. My Catalysts for Change · 43

Part 2

CHAPTER 5. The Model Minority Myth is a Racial Wedge · 57

CHAPTER 6. The Toll of the Model Minority Myth on Asians · 69

Part 3

CHAPTER 7. The U.S. History I Didn't Know · 79

CHAPTER 8. The Facts of Today I Didn't Know · 89

Part 4

CHAPTER 9.	The Problematic "Me"	105
CHAPTER 10.	Colorism in South Asian Culture	111
CHAPTER 11.	The Impact of Casteism and Colonialism on Anti-Blackness	119
CHAPTER 12.	The Media's Influence on Immigrants	129

Part 5

CHAPTER 13.	"Your Baby Won't Be Black"	141
CHAPTER 14.	Growth is Uncomfortable	151
CHAPTER 15.	Conversations with Loved Ones	159

A Word (or, Words) on Ravi	169
Conclusion	173

Acknowledgments	181
Appendix	189

Preface

―――

There are a few things I want to say at the start of your reading journey.

I acknowledge that I cannot speak for the entire South Asian community in America. I can only speak to trends I have observed, lived, and experienced as a person of South Asian descent.

Though this book focuses predominantly on South Asian culture, I include anecdotes involving individuals from the broader Asian community because there are cultural similarities in countries across Asia. There are also certain topics (such as the model minority myth) that necessitate a discussion on Asian culture more broadly. I will include myself in these conversations by using the word "we" because I consider myself a member of the Asian, South Asian, Indian, and Punjabi communities within America. I acknowledge the diversity in cultures and countries of origin within the Asian American diaspora and speak only to areas where I have observed commonalities.

I did my best to articulate my points, but I am still learning how to express myself on a topic that is incredibly challenging, controversial, and charged. I hope my readers know this book was written with an open heart, a deeply uncomfortable degree of vulnerability, and a readiness to receive whatever feedback is needed to broaden my own understanding of the subject. Though I openly discuss my shortcomings and history of prejudice, not everyone is ready to share this degree of vulnerability. For that reason, I have changed the names of some people discussed in this book and modified small details about them to make them unidentifiable.

Many times in the process of writing and revising this book, I wanted to quit. I was so afraid of saying the wrong thing, of phrasing things incorrectly, of putting my foot in my mouth. There was no way I could do this perfectly, and my sense of overwhelm literally kept me awake for nights on end. As my friend Riz pointed out, however, "people are constantly shying away from this work because they're always looking for the right thing to say. If you're trying to make everything perfect before you do this work, you're never going to do it. You have to start with it being messy. Work in drafts, speak in drafts, and let's be willing to give each other grace as we all figure it out. Because if everybody had this right, we wouldn't be here. And there's no way you're going to make everyone happy."

With that said, please know I did my best with this book. It is, like all personal evolution should be, a work in progress.

Thank you for sharing your time and your mental real estate with me during this journey.

Introduction

I lay on my back, acutely aware of the feeling of my bare feet resting in cold metal stirrups. There was a pressure inside my womb and a sharp pain as my doctor prodded against my cervix, mumbling to himself as he examined the image of the tiny bean-sized shape on the screen hanging from the ceiling.

I'd never had a vaginal ultrasound before. I'd never been pregnant before either. It was a time of firsts.

"There's the head," the doctor said, moving his cursor over the larger bean shape on the screen. "And there are its arms, and that portion is the lower body." He wiggled the cursor over the smaller bean shape.

I stared, watching the little shape on the monitor as it jumped.

Mel stood next to me, taking pictures of the ultrasound, before looking down at me with a grin. His face mask covered his actual grin, but I could tell from the way his eyes glittered behind his glasses that he wore a huge smile on that sweet face I loved so deeply.

I looked up at him, happy to see him happy. And then I looked back up at the screen and felt... nothing. I wasn't excited. I wasn't in awe. It was as if I was looking at a video of someone else's baby—curious but disconnected.

As I watched the monitor hanging from the ceiling above me, white vertical lines began appearing in quick succession at the bottom of the screen and a *whooshing* sound filled the room, followed by a rapid *thdump thdump thdump.*

"Is that the heartbeat?" Mel asked excitedly. His voice was slightly muffled by his thick face mask. COVID-19 protocols had been reinstated in Los Angeles, and face masks were again required indoors.

"Yes, that is your baby's heartbeat," the doctor answered, his white brows furrowed in concentration as he took his notes.

My eyes watered as I heard my baby's heartbeat, and a rush of emotion washed over me: first elation, then the sweet thrill of awe, and then... nothing. As quickly as the raw surge of emotion had come, it left me.

And I lay there again, cold, uncomfortable, detached. I winced as the doctor pulled out the device he'd inserted inside of me, then wiped it off and gave me tissues to clean myself up.

"Everything looks good. Let's go into my office so we can talk about the tests we typically run in the first trimester. I'll meet you outside."

He left the room, and Mel helped me off the examining table, kissing my head when I stood. I wiped myself clean of the gel, threw the damp tissues into the trash, and pulled on my leggings.

"We heard the heartbeat," Mel murmured to me, pulling me into his body for a hug.

I rested my cheek against his shirt, wishing I felt more. Wishing I felt excitement. Wishing I felt the joy I knew Mel felt.

But I felt none of those things. This baby was a complete surprise for us. I had just accepted my first corporate job after graduating from business school. I was at the start of a new career.

We weren't financially prepared for a baby, and we had too many things we wanted to do as a couple before we started a family. We weren't ready. *I* wasn't ready.

Regardless, here we were. We were having a baby.

A wave of guilt ran through me as I realized my partner's main emotion was excitement, while mine was visceral fear. Fear that I was unexpectedly having a baby with a man I loved, respected, and adored. But this same man had gone to juvie as a teen and had unresolved trauma from a youth filled with gang violence. And this man was Black. Our baby would be Black and would have an entire lived experience that I, as a Punjabi American woman, could never possibly understand.

How could I, someone who had no idea what it was like to be Black, raise a Black child in a world that was still so filled with racial strife and hatred? It was spring 2021, and the aftermath of George Floyd's murder and the Black Lives Matter movement continued to reverberate through the country. Racial and political divide was still high, and I couldn't see a softening of that divide happening in the near future.

How could I, a woman who had a past marred by anti-Black prejudice and ignorance, raise a Black child to have an unassailable sense of self love and value?

The stark truth was my heart was filled, but it wasn't filled with love or excitement. It was filled with fear, with anxiety, with an overwhelming feeling of "how-the-fuck-do-I-do-this?"

Mel dropped me off at home after my appointment, and before he drove back to work, he kissed me and said, "Thank you for taking care of our baby."

I bit my lip, holding back my tears, and kissed him back. "Thank you for taking care of me," I responded gently and closed the car door, watching him drive away.

I climbed up the steps to our condo and went inside. I changed out of my clothes and pulled on an oversized shirt before climbing into bed and burrowing under the covers. I placed my hand on my lower abdomen, where I knew a tiny human was growing. Where my baby was growing.

I visualized it. This little human. With Mel's smile and my eyes. I imagined Mel holding our baby, nuzzling its neck the way he nuzzled mine. Protecting it, cherishing it, loving it fiercely. And I knew I had to tell our story.

As a South Asian woman, choosing a Black man as my life partner opposed any expectations my conservative Punjabi family could have held for me. In fact, it was counter to any future I could have foreseen for myself, given my personal history of anti-Blackness. But something inside of me shifted when I met Mel, and it didn't matter what my family expected or wanted. I saw my future in his eyes and found my home in his heart.

I closed my eyes, taking in a deep breath. I had a heartbeat in my belly. And that heartbeat was my purpose.

I sent love to that heartbeat in my womb, the little hummingbird rhythm I'd heard earlier that day. It was time to write my book.

Part 1

CHAPTER 1

Growing Up a Brown Girl in a White World

I grew up in the San Fernando Valley, a part of the Los Angeles County in Southern California.

I lived in a predominantly white neighborhood but was raised in a conservative and traditional Punjabi household. During my youth, I rarely interacted with people from the Black community.

Most of the information and knowledge I had about the Black community was from what I saw on television, heard in the news, or learned about from friends or family.

I felt little sympathy or compassion when I read stories about Black people reporting acts of discrimination against them. I believed that, because my family and I had experienced different forms of discrimination and still managed to thrive, there was no excuse for anyone to use discrimination or racism as a way to justify socioeconomic status.

As a brown woman, I struggled to understand the distinction between anti-Black racism and the racism experienced by people who looked like me. To me, racism was racism. Being on the receiving end of it was at times uncomfortable, at times amusing, at times frustrating. And, at times, it was devastating.

I'd received my fair share of racism, in all its various shades and manifestations, from outright racial slurs to the frustrations of cultural appropriation.

In fact, I never quite realized why I felt uncomfortable in yoga studios until I learned about cultural appropriation. It was the core of my unease when I heard yet another white yoga teacher place their hands to their heart and serenely utter, "*Naaahmahhhstaaayyy.*"

To this day, hearing that word at the end of a yoga class makes me cringe.

The word, typically used as a respectful and customary form of greeting amongst Hindi speakers, has become commodified in the Western world of yoga. It is an attempt to add a sense of holiness or reverence to what has essentially become, in the Western world, a workout.

"*Namaste*" is now a word that is plastered on billboards, printed on sweatshirts and T-shirts, and turned into catchphrases (the first time I saw "Nama-slay Bitches!" on a tank top at a yoga studio, I stopped and stared. I was dumbfounded).

Everything about the way this word has been adopted by Western appropriators irritates me. And as petty as it sounds, even the way the word is pronounced at the end of these classes drives me bananas. It is not a challenging word to say, even for non-native Hindi speakers.

If you're choosing to appropriate another person's culture—which is, from my perspective, what is happening when people chant *namaste* or *aum* at the end of a yoga class, snap their fingers and say "NamaSLAY!" or blast hip-hop music in class while wearing shirts with images of the Hindu god Ganesh on them—please at least *try* to learn how to say it properly.

But the irritation I feel at the various ways yogic and Ayurvedic traditions have been appropriated by Western culture (don't get me started on turmeric-based lattes and beverages) is heightened when I come face-to-face with it in my personal life, with people who remain stubborn in their ignorance.

My dad's white friend, Uncle Mike, once cracked a joke about a colleague named Vikram. We were at dinner at a restaurant in Phoenix, Arizona, during the summer of 2020.

"This guy, he had one of those Indian names that's hard to pronounce," Uncle Mike had said. "Vikram or Vikroom or something ridiculous like that."

I'd stared at him and said, "I'm not sure why 'Vikram' is any harder to pronounce than the name 'Victor.'"

Uncle Mike laughed, thinking I was joking, and pushed forth with his commentary.

My parents finished their meals quickly, and we left dinner early.

We no longer talk to Uncle Mike. My parents and I had hit capacity with his ignorance and decided to allow the relationship to fizzle. The summer of 2020 saw the exit of many people from our lives.

The Beautiful Chaos of Being Punjabi American

As a thirty-three-year-old, brown-skinned Punjabi woman, exchanges like the one described involving Uncle Mike aren't uncommon to me.

My experience growing up in America has been a colorful one. Painful and isolating but also at times enlightening and interesting.

To this day, I am often asked, "Where are you from?"

My response is usually, "California."

To which the typical reply is, "No, where are you *from*?"

"The Los Angeles area."

"Okay, but where are your *parents* from?"

"Well, my mother was born in Nairobi, Kenya, and my dad is from Jartauli."

I don't know why I can't just say, "I am Punjabi American."

I make things difficult for the other person and steep myself in my expectation of semantical propriety. In my mind, they should be asking, "What is your ethnicity?" That is a question I'm happy to answer because where I am *from* is different than the *culture* within which I was born. And it is not tied into my racial identity.

I am *from* Los Angeles (or the San Fernando Valley, to be more specific), but my ethnicity is Punjabi. I am a brown woman who was born into a Punjabi Sikh family and grew up in a traditionally conservative Punjabi Sikh community.

The thing is, for me, growing up in an Indian household steeped in the mores and customs of Punjab was both beautiful and confusing. My childhood was a kaleidoscope of color and sound. I was constantly surrounded by *bhangra* music, vibrant colors, fragrant foods, and the endless chatter of a large family of about twenty people all living together under one roof.

Indian culture is one of community, and extended families are the norm. It is not uncommon to find grandparents, parents, cousins, uncles, aunts, and siblings all residing under one roof. It takes a village to raise a family, and your village becomes your family. The bustle and chaos of growing up in an extended family was oftentimes very comforting. I loved dancing through the house as my dad and uncles sang aloud to Jazzy B songs while my younger brother shoved Indian snacks into his mouth, watching my mother roll *rotis* for dinner. Cousins stumbled over each other as we all played, and the house was in a constant state of disarray with all the moving bodies and activity.

Unfortunately, the beauty of my culture's food, language, clothes, and customs was tainted by the backward beliefs of the villages from which my family came. I was admonished for getting too fat while having deep-fried *laddoos* shoved into my mouth. I was told to "sit down and be quiet" while also being told to "speak louder, I can't hear you over this noise."

From a young age, I questioned my own value because I was born female (Indian culture in general values males over females), and I noted how differently my grandmother treated my brothers compared to how she treated me. I feared and hated my father for his alcoholic rages and temper, but I adored and loved him for his humor and affection.

My relationship with my mother was a source of confusion for me as well. A woman who was routinely victim to my father's violent outbursts and the abuses of a judgmental and jealous sister-in-law, my young mother sometimes channeled her own pain into aggression toward us.

As a child, on any given day I could be bullied and shown affection in the same breath, unaware that love and affection did not need to be intertwined with emotional and mental abuse.

The Experience of Being an "Other"

My sense of confusion regarding my identity and value escalated when I left the comfort of my brown family and entered the white world of school. I had to learn to straddle the line of two worlds: my Punjabi home and the American world outside of it.

There was a brief transitory period in preschool, however, during which I was blissfully unaware of my otherness.

I remember being three years old and crying as we dropped my older brother off at school. I wanted to stay too! I wanted to play and read and learn and grow.

Except, I didn't really speak much English. Nonetheless, I persisted in my requests to stay with my brother until I was finally, one day, dropped off with my brother and allowed to join the preschool. It was almost a year before I spoke a word to my classmates or teacher, communicating mostly with laughter and smiles and by pointing my fingers and hands.

As I grew older and entered elementary school, things began to change. I began to notice my classmates all appeared different from me. I had more body hair than they did. My skin was so much darker than theirs, and their mothers packed different foods in their lunch boxes than my mother packed in mine. My lunches had stronger smells and gave classmates yet another reason to tease me.

In fact, one of my favorite lunches brought me a lot of attention: my mother's French toast. My family "Indianified" French toast, and we did it by doing what we do to almost everything we cook; we added cumin.

It was a long time before I learned the nuances between different types of cuisine, as my family's habit of adding large amounts of cumin to almost everything made it difficult to differentiate between Italian and Mexican and Mediterranean foods. Thus, when cooked at home, all these cuisines tasted vaguely the same. And because I mostly ate at home until my teenage years, my introduction to non-Indianified cuisines was a little alarming.

The first time I had French toast at a white classmate's house, I was genuinely mystified. "Can I have ketchup?" I asked when my classmate's mother handed me syrup.

She looked horrified. "You want ketchup? With the French toast?"

You see, instead of cinnamon and vanilla, we made our egg batter with salt, pepper, cumin, and savory spices. We dipped the bread in the batter, fried it, and served it with ketchup, hot sauce, or chutney. This is what French toast was to me my entire life. It was my favorite lunch treat, and I would dance a jig of joy when my mother packed it for me during my younger years.

I did not realize the impact this culinary twist had on my observant classmates until I was in the eighth grade. Prior to that year, I had to switch schools multiple times due to bullying. My religious studies teacher in the sixth grade adamantly held that I would go to hell unless I converted to Christianity and made it known to the entire class that my soul was in jeopardy. I was placed in a different school for the seventh grade, and then, because of severe bullying post 9/11, my parents put me into yet another school in the eighth grade.

On the first day of eighth grade at my new school, a girl who looked vaguely familiar pointed at me.

"Oh my gosh, I know you! *You're the girl who ate French toast with ketchup in kindergarten!*" she declared.

The students around us laughed, and my face burned hot in embarrassment.

My "otherness" posed a problem all through school. I remember when little boys would run up to me on the playground in the fourth grade and point at me.

"You worship cows. I worship Jesus. Moooo!" They'd taunt me, make faces, and laugh.

When this first happened to me, my nine-year-old self was genuinely perplexed. I am not Hindu. My family is Sikh. It is the Hindu culture that specifically does not consume beef. Plus, Hindus hold the cow sacred but do not generally "worship" cows. Cows provide their flesh, their milk, their hides, and their dung for human comfort and are therefore revered for their generosity and gentle spirit. Why is that something to be mocked?

In the seventh grade, the tragedy of 9/11 occurred. I remember walking into my parents' room early that morning before school, seeing an image of an airplane crashing into buildings as my father watched, his face crestfallen and scared. I was a little confused by his expression, since I thought he was watching a movie. It would be some time until I understood exactly what happened that day. And what it meant for our country. It didn't take long for me to realize what it meant for my people.

The weeks and months following 9/11 were terrifying for my young self. I was routinely harassed at school for being brown. "Terrorist!" the white girls at school would jeer at me. I waited for my parents after school one day, and a group of white girls surrounded me. One pushed me to the floor, and they all spat on me. "Go home to your own country," they sneered.

But this was my country. I was born here. It was the only country I knew.

We began receiving phone calls. A man in our community had been shot in the head at the gas station he owned. He was a Sikh, and he'd been wearing a turban. Because of his turban, someone thought he was Muslim and decided he didn't deserve to be alive anymore. For years after that, my grandfather began wearing baseball caps over his hair when in public, reserving his turban for community and religious gatherings.

Sikhs across the country were assaulted, attacked, and killed (Basu 2016). I learned what it meant to be called the daughter of a "raghead," and my parents had to tell me why my classmates referred to me as a "sand nigger."

But the bullying wasn't just relegated to my religion and skin tone. My hair created problems. Mostly because I had it everywhere. Even my brothers called me a gorilla, as puberty gifted me with body hair on my lower back, the length of my thighs, legs, arms, and, to my horror, on my face.

I remember in the seventh grade, a small-framed boy would stare at me often. *Does he like me?* I would wonder to myself, never having been the object of any male's fascination before.

One day, my heart flew into my throat as I watched this boy march boldly up to me. *Maybe he's going to tell me he likes me!*

He stopped in front of me, crossed his arms, and demanded, "Why do you have a mustache?"

I was so surprised, I couldn't help but respond to him.

"I don't know," I answered honestly.

The Discomfort of Straddling Two Worlds

I was incredibly different in both appearance and culture from my classmates during my preteen and teen years, so I did my damnedest to assimilate. But as I assimilated into that English-speaking white world, my "Punjabi-ness" became diluted.

By the time I entered college, I fit into neither world. I felt like I was floating, lost, without an anchor to ground me anywhere.

During my first year of college, small things were said to me that grated against my sense of self.

"You're prettier than most Indians I've met," one white girl told me after she came to a group project slightly inebriated.

"Your skin was fair, and that's what first caught my eye about you," my Punjabi ex-husband, Ravinder (Ravi for short), told me a few months after we first met.

In fact, Ravi would gently admonish me for staying out in the sun. "You're going to get dark," he'd tell me in concern.

"You look like a *gori*," he'd say lovingly during our evening winter walks, after I'd spend months avoiding the sun in fear of getting "too dark."

"*Gori*" is the Punjabi word for "white girl" or "fair-skinned girl."

I would develop anxiety if I became too tan during hot summer days as I crossed the large UCLA campus from one class to the next.

Fast forward a handful of years, and I collected a series of experiences that made me realize I had no sense of self identity anymore.

In the yoga world, I was supposed to be "good" at yoga. After all, "my people" were the ones who "invented it." My hair was "supposed" to be long and thick, and it surprised people to find my hair was fine and thin.

My hair does not now, nor has it ever, fit the standard of what Indian hair "should" be.

When I ended my marriage to Ravi, I cut ties with my Punjabi community and moved across the country to distance myself from my family. I could no longer stand the self-hate my community perpetuated within me.

"Be fair skinned, be skinny, ASSIMILATE but also don't forget your roots and make sure you know how to cook and clean and be a good housewife BUT ALSO GET AN EDUCATION AND BE SUCCESSFUL. Become a doctor or a dentist or a lawyer or an engineer." It exhausted me.

Over the last handful of years, things have been evolving for brown girls. I'm seeing more diverse representation on television screens, more brown women advocating for themselves and starting their own careers and businesses, marrying later in life, pushing back against the customs and mores that stifled us for so long.

More people are talking about race than ever before, and I no longer resent my skin tone the way I did when I was young.

I'm better able to handle racial ignorance directed toward me. I don't internalize it anymore. I no longer question my value when people say hurtful things.

But I do still struggle with the ignorance I face. It still grates at me. My white roommate in New York was a blonde, green-eyed woman who'd grown up in Montauk. I knew her casually when we decided to become roommates, and our casual friendship didn't last long. She would say things to me that would silence me with their baffling absurdity.

"Oh my god, can you please stop talking Indian at my dog," she'd yell from her room while I chattered to her Labrador in Punjabi as he followed me around while I cooked.

"Are you going to put curry in my cheesecake?" she asked warily when I asked if I could use my favorite spices while we baked for an upcoming party. I was thinking nutmeg, cinnamon, cloves—she heard me say "spice" and assumed I wanted cumin and curry powder in her dessert.

Before I met Mel, dating could be frustrating. I would hear things like, "I've never been on a date with an Indian before" or "I'm assuming you like spicy food, but you should know I don't" or "Don't your parents want you to have an arranged marriage?"

I was never quite sure how to respond. When I was sassy, people got offended. If I was witty, people got uncomfortable and looked guilty. When I remained quiet, I hated myself.

There are certain times when I feel helpless in the face of ignorance because I realize that certain stereotypes are in fact true. My parents *do* own 7-Elevens. There *are* a lot of Indian taxi drivers. We *do* shake our heads side to side when we talk.

So when people crack jokes, "Oh, I bet your parents have that 7-Eleven money," I don't know what to say. Because, yes, they do have that 7-Eleven money. And yes, your clothes will smell if you visit my mother's house because fried onions seasoned with turmeric is a deeply intense odor that will haunt you and your hair and clothes for days.

Reading these stories in a book about anti-Blackness in the South Asian community may leave you wondering, "So what? Why do we care about any of these stories?" I included them because my experiences growing up as a brown girl in a white world deeply informed my understanding of racism in this country. They were the root cause of my "whataboutmeism," why I couldn't grasp why anti-Black racism was any different from what I myself experienced.

It was why I remained ignorant of my prejudice for so long. If I was also on the receiving end of discrimination and prejudice, how could it be possible for me to exhibit the same discrimination and prejudice toward someone else?

CHAPTER 2

The Roots of My Prejudice

"Ugh, I'm so tired of seeing these people use food stamps to buy Doritos and ice cream. Like, you're getting free money and then you get sick and use taxpayer money when you get your government subsidized health care."

I listened to one of my best friends on the other side of the phone, nodding my head vigorously as I leaned back in my bed, idly toying with the edges of the book I'd rested in my lap.

The white cover of the book was graced by a blue sculpture of the Titan Atlas, holding a hollow globe on his shoulder. The book was the second my friend and I had read together as part of a two-person book club we'd started during our final year of college. *Atlas Shrugged*, Ayn Rand's best-known work, was all the tinder we needed to fuel our self-righteous judgement of Americans using EBT and unemployment.

"I know, right," I agreed, rolling my eyes. "It makes me so angry. They're literally being given free money. They can learn how to take care of themselves. My parents are immigrants. They came here with nothing, and they worked hard for everything they have. There's no excuse." I grimaced when I saw how dark my hand looked against the white background of the book cover.

I'd spent too much time in the sun that summer. I was getting too tanned. I shook off my pang of anxiety at the contrast between my skin and the book cover and continued. "Everything in this book is so on point. We live in a free country where anyone can be anything. I think people just make excuses and don't want to do the hard work it takes to build a better life."

My friend, a white girl I'd met at my private Catholic high school, agreed with me as I ranted, and then continued talking about her frustrations as a tutor helping people prepare for their GEDs. Her students were predominantly from low-income, minority communities.

I listened intently, agreeing wholeheartedly with her judgments, ignorant to the reality of both of our self-righteous myopia.

It would take me almost a full decade for the truth to hit me, for the cracks in the foundations of the narratives I'd been fed my entire life—narratives I blindly accepted—to appear. And even then, after years of educating myself, it would take me falling in love with a Black man to truly realize the layers of my own prejudice and the depth of my ignorance on the systematic and systemic oppression Black people in America have experienced and continue to experience in this country.

Exposed to the belief systems and values of my Punjabi community in Southern California, I was raised to believe that hard work, education, and discipline were the only things people needed in order to experience upward socioeconomic mobility. We were in charge of our own destinies, and anyone who said otherwise was sitting in a hot shit pile of excuses.

It was unequivocal, this message that the American Dream was attainable for all. My father, born in a village in India, was brought to America as a child by my grandparents. My grandfather, an engineer who would eventually work for one of the world's largest defense contractors, was an educated man who moved to America on his own before bringing his family to a country that was, in the minds of most people in my father's village, the holy grail for success and opportunity.

My father arrived in Los Angeles when he was eleven years old. He, like his mother and two younger siblings, spoke no English. My father and his siblings struggled to understand why the children at school mocked them. Together, the four of them learned to navigate a new landscape, a new world, and a new way of living.

Mercilessly teased and bullied in school, my father and uncle eventually cut off their *juras*, a wrapped topknot young Sikh boys wear openly that eventually becomes wrapped in a turban as they enter adulthood. They listened to rock music to learn English. They discovered pizza and cable television. They assimilated.

Over the years, my father was racially profiled, jeered at, mocked, and ridiculed for the color of his skin. Still, he found success. My grandfather invested his earnings into a 7-Eleven at the behest of my grandmother, who sought her own path in this new country. It was the 70s, and as a brown woman with no education, my grandmother's career options were limited. But if she owned a store, she'd never have to worry about being hired or fired. So my grandfather used his savings from his engineering job to acquire a 7-Eleven.

Eventually, one store turned into two, two turned into three, and three turned into my father making a handsome income as a 7-Eleven owner at the tender age of twenty-one.

And from here were sown the seeds that built the narrative I was fed from an early age: No matter what cards you are given in life, if you put in the time and energy to learn how to play them right (and then have the discipline to actually play them), you will find success.

The theme song of my upbringing seemed straightforward: get an education, stay out of trouble, and nothing will stand in your way.

Also inherent in my upbringing was an undercurrent of judgment toward anyone who didn't follow the prescribed playbook—judgment toward the members of our own community as well as toward the outside world.

Woven into that judgment was a thick thread of racism, both overt and covert. Anti-Blackness, more specifically, was something I'd been exposed to at a very young age. Actual exposure to the Black community itself, however, was incredibly limited.

The messages about Black people that circulated in my community were, as I look back at them, steeped in negativity. Black people were lazy, violent, cheaters, uneducated, and unreliable. They joined gangs, caused trouble, did drugs, and most of the men ended up in prison. These stereotypes were readily accepted by most of the people in my community (I say "most" because I cannot speak for all, though I never came across anyone who openly disagreed or spoke out against these stereotypes, and I had family spread across America, Canada, England, and India).

From a young age, I was taught to fear and judge Black people. I recall a moment as a child when my aunt was laughing, telling my mother about an exchange she had with my younger cousin at the grocery store.

My young cousin saw a Black woman at the register, pointed, and said, "Look, mom, it's a chocolate person!"

The woman, according to my aunt, looked over and said, "Excuse me?"

My aunt pulled my cousin by the arm out of the store and back into the car. There was no education, no conversation provided to my younger cousin about different cultures and races. Instead, the exchange became a funny story to share over *chaa*.

When I struggled with bullying at school that centered around my own skin color, my father would try to comfort me. "Human beings are like cookies," he said. "When God took us out of the oven after making us, he saw that the white people weren't cooked properly, the Black people were cooked too much, and the brown people were cooked *just* right."

While I grew up thinking this story was a sweet memory of my father comforting me, it took me over two decades to realize how harmful this way of explaining race to a child truly is.

As I grew older, I wasn't particularly aware of my family's prejudice. It was just a part of my life, as integrated into my existence as waking up every morning.

Living in America as immigrants should have provided my community with a deep-rooted understanding of the minority experience, an understanding infused with compassion and empathy for a shared struggle.

Unfortunately, it didn't. I was brought up with the belief that white people and Punjabi people were the only kinds of people I should really spend time with. Every other race and ethnicity had *something* that made it, somehow, too different. Black Americans? They committed crimes and made no money. Mexicans? They did your landscaping and sometimes construction. East Asians? They rip you off at the market downtown, but they *do* have tasty food (excellent use of spices). Persians and Armenians weren't to be trusted (apparently they played tricks during business dealings). Even South Indians were categorized differently. They were darker and looked different from us Punjabi people, so we were separated from them too.

This is what I was taught, and if no one explicitly taught me, it is what I observed. Even after 9/11, when we had the opportunity to come together in love and support of the human spirit, my immediate Punjabi community continued to support beliefs about entire groups of people based exclusively on phenotype and the negative stereotypes accompanying these phenotypes.[1]

When I was seventeen, I was admitted to a reputable university in Southern California. On our way to the university tour, my father informed me that a Punjabi woman he knew had married a Black man. I had been shocked when he told me, and he shared the gossip surrounding her decision. However, the university tour began, and we quickly dropped the conversation. Toward the end of the tour, my father opened his arms wide, as if to embrace the scenery around him, and said, "Look at all of this. You can come here, get an amazing opportunity, and ruin it by being with a Black man. Or by becoming a social worker."

I don't really know which was worse to him: being with a Black man or suffering the limited earning potential of being a social worker.

---

1. "Phenotype" refers to a person's observable traits (such as skin color, height, facial features, or eye color).

Years later, after I was married to Ravi, a conversation with my ex-mother-in-law stood out to me. She had discovered her Punjabi daughter was in a relationship with a white man, and she accepted it with little disgruntlement. As I sat on the floor in front of her so she could brush my hair, I said, "It seems like you're okay that he's white. But what if he was Mexican? Black? Muslim?"

Her response remains strong in my mind today.

"Oh, no, no. Black? Never. Maybe a Mexican would be okay because they are family oriented. But they don't make much money or have very good jobs. Never a Muslim. And never a Black man. White is better, if she isn't with a Punjabi man."

I remember sitting next to her and nodding. Though at the time her response was obvious to me, it also made me uncomfortable, but I couldn't exactly articulate why. To me racism was violence, aggression, or whispers in public spaces. It was not a conversation on a sofa, surrounded by loved ones.

I was still married to Ravi then, a man who was incredibly prejudiced and strongly influenced by the prejudices within our Punjabi community as a whole. It was not until I left that relationship that the depths of his prejudice, and the prejudice that surrounded me growing up, became apparent.

I remember comments Ravi's cousin made after seeing a pretty Black actress on the screen while we were all lounging in front of the television: "She's hot, but she's dark."

I had agreed and added, "She's not naturally pretty, though, because that isn't her actual hair that's sewn all over her head." My sister-in-law nodded, and we joked about how much money we'd be able to make if we sold our hair to be made into weaves. Not only was my comment ignorant but I also had no idea if this actress actually had a sew-in weave. I just assumed she did because she was Black.

I think of it all now, and I feel physically ill. I clearly participated in these conversations. I perpetuated the prejudice. This type of thinking was all I knew. My little bubble of myopia and ignorance was strengthened because the people I was surrounded by were from essentially the same bubble.

My First Love (Was Anti-Black… and I Didn't Do Anything about It)

Despite the bumps I experienced growing up as a brown person in a predominantly white area, I blossomed in college. I felt more confident in my skin as I put more attention into my workouts and image, and the bookish vibe I had emitted my entire life moved aside for a more fun, exciting, coming-of-age version of myself. Boys began to show interest in me, and I basked in the attention.

During my first semester, I remember going home to see my mother and telling her, quite seriously, "Mum, I want you to know something. I'll probably end up with a white man."

My mother's face fell, and she said, "Why would you say that to me? Are you seeing someone?"

I shrugged my shoulders and said, "No. But I just don't want to deal with brown guys. So just be prepared." Looking back at that exchange, it never once crossed my mind that there would be any other race or ethnicity to consider for partnership. If I wasn't going to date an Indian man, then my only remaining default option was a white man. Never mind I was too shy and insecure at that point to date any man, but if my future self was going to be in a relationship it would be with a white man.

My first kiss wouldn't happen until the following year,

a few months after my nineteenth birthday. Much to the delight of my mother, it was with a tall, handsome Punjabi boy who was pressing full steam ahead toward a career in medicine. He came from a successful, prestigious family. He spoke our language, was an active member of our faith, and was every Punjabi mother's dream come true.

This man, Ravi, was my first love and would eventually become my husband. The relationship consumed me. So much so that the red flags that waved brightly in my face wouldn't truly be processed until years later.

I remember the first time I heard him refer to a Black person as a "nig," my head whipped over to look at him.

"What did you just say?" I demanded.

"Look at that nig," he said, pointing at a young Black man crossing the street. "His pants are about to fall down."

I watched the man cross the street, noting his sagging pants before turning back to my boyfriend.

"Ravi, don't say that. It's not a nice word."

"What are you talking about?" he scoffed. "He dresses like a nig, so he is a nig."

Despite my protestations, he never stopped using that word. The first time he referred to a young Black child as a "niglet," my eyes watered and my face got hot.

"Don't say that around me. I don't like it. It's so mean. You shouldn't be saying it at all," I said angrily.

He and his cousin laughed uproariously, completely taken with their fusion of the racial slur with the word "piglet."

As much as I protested and as upset as his language made me, it never upset me enough to break up with him. I'm not sure *why*—maybe it was the assumption that all Indians thought this way. I think, though, at the time I didn't truly grasp how *harmful* the language was, that it represented something much deeper and darker than a careless word thrown around casually amongst family members.

I was also the only person who ever really protested when the word was used. His cousins thought the language was funny. His sister thought the language was funny. No one around us, other than me, had an issue with it. A part of me thought I was being overly sensitive, that I couldn't take a joke. I didn't realize that the normalization of racist jokes continues to perpetuate harmful and toxic views of entire groups of people.

I would argue and speak out against outright racist jokes or comments I found repulsive—but the softer, quieter comments I allowed to pass. And I never challenged the stereotypes or narratives my community held against Black people. I realize now, looking back at the person I used to be, that it is because I was also anti-Black. I just hadn't come to terms with it yet.

The summer between Ravi's first and second years of medical school, we found a little apartment in Westwood, California. It was a short walk from the laboratory within which Ravi would conduct research for a clinical assignment he'd been given. One hot afternoon, he came home from the lab with a troubled look upon his face.

"Something weird happened today," he said. "I think I messed up in front of Jon." Jon was a graduate student who also worked in the lab with Ravi.

"What do you mean?" I asked him.

"Well, during lunch, we decided to run out and grab some food. We were sitting in Jon's car at a stoplight. I saw this *kahla*[2] walk by, and he was doing this weird dance. I started laughing and was like, 'Wow, look at that nig.'"

---

2. *Kahla* means "black" in the Punjabi language. It is the word Indians use to describe Black people. *Kahle*, pronounced kal-ay, is literally the plural form of the word *kahla*.

I cringed, as I often did when I heard that word. And I immediately felt embarrassed. Not just for Ravi, and that he'd be so careless to use that word around someone outside of the family, but also for myself—embarrassed I was with someone who would use that word so easily.

Ravi frowned deeply and said, "And then Jon turned to me and was like, 'Ravi, are you racist?' And I was like, 'Nah bro, why would you say that?' And he said that it sounded like I was racist because I said 'nig.' I'm not racist, right?"

He looked at me with concern etched into his forehead.

"I mean, I tell you that using that word isn't nice," I replied. "And I keep telling you to stop saying it. I can't believe you said it in front of someone else."

"But just because I say it, it doesn't make me racist, right?"

"No," I said, wrapping my arms around his waist to comfort him. "It doesn't make you racist." *But is that true? I'd wondered. Is he racist? Am I racist for telling him he's not?* I honestly didn't know.

"Good," he said. "I don't want Jon to think I'm racist."

Even then, I noted he wasn't so much concerned about being racist himself. He was just concerned *someone else* would think he was racist.

As I think back on that time in my life, I remember how much I struggled to push back on problematic and racist things people in my community would say. The fact is that prejudiced and judgmental thinking had become normalized for me.

I was inundated with messaging that light skin was superior to dark skin and that all it took to be successful in America was hard work and discipline. This messaging translated over into how I, and the community within which I was raised, perceived the Black community. If we, a community of color, could succeed and thrive, then racism and discrimination were not valid reasons to explain the struggles of the Black community. This messaging was compounded by the media we consumed, which validated our prejudiced viewpoints.

Because we were people of color, we didn't challenge our problematic views against Black people. We also experienced racism, didn't we? What about us? If we could survive racism and thrive, why couldn't "they"?

CHAPTER 3

A Blue-Eyed Boy and *The Vagina Monologues*

A handful of years after devouring *Atlas Shrugged*, I found myself in an auditorium at Columbia University, prepared to watch *The Vagina Monologues*, a play written by playwright Eve Ensler. The play is comprised of stories based on the actual, lived experiences of women and led to the birth of "V-Day," a global grassroots movement to end violence against women and girls. The play is episodic, consisting of stories including topics like consensual and nonconsensual sex, genital mutilation, gender identity, vaginal hygiene, sex work, and body image.

This rendition of *The Vagina Monologues* was particularly controversial, as the entire cast was comprised of women of color. The controversy lay in the fact that auditions were only open to women who identified as women of color. If you were not a woman of color, you wouldn't even be considered for an audition.

As a young woman of color, I was curious as to the "why" of this decision. At this point, my otherness was so deeply ingrained in me, had impacted so much of my life, and had isolated me from so many of my white peers that I didn't understand why other women who looked like me would want their otherness to be spotlighted, highlighted, and brought quite literally to the center of the stage.

As I sat in the darkened auditorium watching the play, I was captivated and entranced the entire time, fascinated by the stories and talents of the young women storytellers… until a young Black woman came to the stage. She grabbed her crotch, and shouted, "This country was built on the backs of Black women, was built through the labor of Black pussy."

I vividly recall shifting uncomfortably in my chair, looking around me to see if anyone else felt the energy on the stage become combative.

I couldn't see the faces of my fellow audience members, so I forced myself to pay attention to what was happening on stage. The woman spoke of racism against Black people, of oppression. She demanded reparations, acknowledgment for the fact that "this country" would not exist if it had not broken the backs of her Black ancestors. As she spoke, my frustration grew. I didn't want to hear this woman complaining anymore. The other stories of the play spoke to me: stories of identity confusion, of sexual frustration, and of sexual assault. They gave me goose bumps. But that final story? It just felt like another Black person complaining about racism and wanting reparations.

Looking back on it, my discomfort was rooted in willful ignorance and the prejudice I'd been taught my entire life. As I said before: I was taught that if you worked hard, you'd achieve your dreams. You wouldn't need reparations. You'd get to your end goal on your own. The people who complained were just making excuses.

I endured the rest of the play and went home, disappointed in my experience.

The next day, I took the Megabus from downtown Manhattan to Washington, DC, where Ravi (my boyfriend-turned-fiancé) waited to pick me up from the station.

I was exhausted by the time I arrived, and I was looking forward to showering, putting on my pajamas, and spending the rest of the evening eating homemade food with Ravi and his roommate, Joshua.

Joshua was a white Jewish man from Alaska. He had a slight build, a wiry frame, a head full of curly blonde hair and the bluest eyes I've ever seen on a person. He was one of Ravi's only friends in medical school, and they bonded over their love of the outdoors and traditional Indian food.

Joshua is, to this day, the only white person I've ever met who would eat *achaar* straight out of the jar.

He explored other countries and cuisines voraciously, and part of my love for his company was the interest he displayed in learning more about other cultures. He was curious about everything and had a pure and open heart.

He was a kind and gentle man, one who only raised his voice when excited or surprised. I had never seen him get angry, and even his frustration was transient. He spent his energy seeking solutions rather than ruminating on obstacles.

That night, we all ate dinner together, laughing as Joshua shared his most recent experience with the dating app he'd downloaded a few weeks before. We discussed science, medicine, and law. It was a fun evening, but we retired early because Ravi had an early morning the next day.

As I lay in bed next to Ravi, I was too energized to sleep. I heard Joshua in the kitchen, and I crept out of bed to see what he was doing.

He was organizing the fridge, taking out containers of food and emptying the contents into the trash before moving to the sink to wash the glass dishes.

He grinned at me when he saw me standing in the kitchen doorway, and I walked over and leaned against the counter to watch him as he washed the dishes.

"I forgot to ask you how that play you saw was," he said. "Ravi told me you went to see a super weird play last night."

"Oh yeah." I rolled my eyes. "It was so freaking weird. It was pretty good overall, but the second half was just really intense and unexpected. It was *The Vagina Monologues*, but it was done only with women of color. It was a little annoying to be honest."

"Why was it annoying?" he asked. He scrubbed dried food off the inside of his food container with a soapy sponge.

"I just got irritated with all the complaining at the end. Like 'I demand reparations, my people are poor, we have no opportunities,' blah blah blah kind of thing."

Joshua kept scrubbing, but his eyebrows furrowed deeply. "What do you mean, they were complaining? Reparations?"

"Yeah, at the end there was this Black girl, and she was really intense and was saying how America was built on the backs of Black people and they were oppressed and wanted reparations."

"Okay… but is that complaining, or was that just her telling the truth? I don't know a lot about the play but isn't it something about women sharing true stories of their lives?"

"I mean, yeah," I said. "But to me, it's like, okay, I experience racism. I've experienced it my whole life. My dad came to America with nothing and worked his butt off. I don't think experiencing racism is something that's unique to Black people. Indians experience racism, and we don't demand reparations."

Joshua began rinsing his dishes. "Yeah, but being an immigrant is pretty different than being a Black person who was born in America. And reparations are specifically for people impacted by slavery. That's doesn't include immigrants. They're for Black people. So it wouldn't make sense for you to demand reparations."

My face got hot with anger. I pushed off the counter and planted my feet, still facing him.

"I don't think my experiences with racism are any less harmful than a Black person's," I said firmly. "I've been spit on. I've been called horrible names. Sikhs were killed after 9/11, and my dad has been harassed by police officers because of the color of his skin."

"I mean, it's not fair that Black people experience racism," I continued. "But it's also not unique to them. I feel like most of them just complain and don't do anything. Like, my friend worked in AmeriCorps, and she would tell me that most of the people she worked with only met with her so they could get free government money. And then even the ones on food stamps wouldn't buy healthy food, they would just buy junk."

"I mean, I don't get why any of that is relevant," he said, irritation in his voice. He rinsed the final dish and ran water over the sponge, squeezing it to rinse out the soap. He put the sponge down and faced me.

I panicked slightly at Joshua's obvious irritation. My heart beat a little faster. As a people-pleaser, I despised making people irritated or annoyed with me. But I needed him to understand my point.

"It's relevant because it's frustrating when people complain about their situation and don't do anything about it.

This is America. If you just work hard, there's no excuse for not improving your life. My dad started with nothing, and he's provided for his family. My dad came to this country and built his life from the ground up. He achieved the American Dream through hard work and dedication. No one just handed it to him. He'd wake up at 4:00 a.m. every day and worked weekends. Everything my parents did was to provide a good life for us, so we could go to school and make sure we did the same for our children. Why do Black people think they deserve anything more than what we get?"

Joshua's face tensed as he listened to me. "Your dad isn't Black. It's different being Black. This is America. I get that you've experienced racism, but being Black in America is different from being an immigrant. You have to think of Black history in America."

"You're talking about slavery?"

"Well, yeah," Joshua said, shrugging. I could feel him pulling back from the conversation as my voice got more intense.

I stopped myself from rolling my eyes. "Slavery was a long time ago. It's 2013. At this point, you have to take ownership over your own life."

Joshua shook his head. "You don't get it. It's not about that. It's about the oppression and the lack of opportunities that continued even after slavery ended. It's about the generations of people who have been oppressed, and the fact that entire communities were basically subjugated to the outskirts of society and don't get access to the same resources as people who aren't Black."

I listened to him, and my anger rose. I was done with this conversation. He wasn't getting it. He was discounting me. What about me? What about my family? What about all the horrible things my community faced because they didn't look like the white man? *What about the racism I had experienced, the traumas I had suffered?*

"Okay, well, I'm going to bed," I said.

Joshua's face tightened with disappointment. I left the kitchen, my face hot and my shoulders stiff. Even now, years later, I remember my unease and shame. He had triggered something inside of me, and my anxiety clawed its way up through my chest and throat. It burned my eyes.

I went back into the bedroom and crawled into bed next Ravi. He slept soundly, his deep breaths uninterrupted by my fidgeting.

I don't know why that conversation upset me so much. It wasn't just my frustration with Joshua for not seeing my point of view, it was also confusing to me that someone would so strongly disagree with my perspective when they had no idea what it was like to grow up in my skin. To compound this, up until this point in my life I'd never met someone who didn't hold the same conservative viewpoints held by my family about work ethic and opportunity in America.

My Jewish and white friends at Columbia all held views similar to my family's. Ravi and his family held similar views to my family's as well. My high school friends, who were themselves children of immigrants from Iran, Syria, Korea, Vietnam, and Taiwan, all also held similar views. As did my cousins in England and my uncle in Vancouver. My relatives and family friends: all of us engaging in a giant snowball cycle of confirmation bias.

This was the first time I had ever been confronted with pushback. It was the first time someone had told me that while my experiences weren't invalid, they weren't the same as those of Black people. It was the first time someone had looked me in the eyes and told me Black people were specifically maltreated, and it was that maltreatment at the root of the disparities in opportunities and income the Black community experienced in America. It wasn't just a matter of "work hard, achieve your dreams." It was a matter of generational trauma and targeted anti-Black racism and oppression.

It is my shame, even today, that instead of allowing that conversation with Joshua to propel me into change, I simply tucked it away, deep inside of me. My denial was so great, and it was validated when I spoke to Ravi about the conversation the next day.

"Man, Josh is wild. Ignore him. He gets into his hippie-dippie ideas sometimes. I agree with everything you said," he told me, when I expressed my anxiety over my conversation with Joshua. Comforted, I nestled even further into my denial. Later that day, I went to Joshua's room and knocked on his door.

"Hi, Josh," I said, almost shyly.

"SanDEEP!" he said enthusiastically, almost shouting out the second syllable in my name. "Check out this new song I wrote." He began moving his fingers quickly over the strings of his acoustic guitar.

I smiled and interrupted his playing, "That sounds good, but I really wanted to just come in here and apologize to you for getting so intense last night."

"Oh, don't worry about it," he said, continuing his strumming. "It's all good."

I pressed on. "I know we don't agree on everything, but I don't want you to think I didn't hear you and don't want you to have a negative view of me or anything."

"Nah, we're cool. Don't even think about it. Wait, I wanted to show you this new *achaar* I bought from this Asian store I found a couple of days ago." He tossed his guitar onto his comforter and leapt off his bed, rushing by me to head into the kitchen. I followed him, shaking my head, wondering how a man who seemingly had the attention span of a squirrel could have elicited so much anxiety from me the night before.

It would be years before my "what-about-me" mentality toward anti-Black racism in America would be challenged again. This time, my reckoning would come in the form of a small, fiercely loving Black woman named Sabina.

CHAPTER 4

My Catalysts for Change

Meeting Sabina

The conversation I had with Joshua was the first time my worldview as it pertained to race was ever truly challenged. After that late night exchange in the basement kitchen of Ravi's apartment, years passed before I would come face-to-face with my own anti-Blackness.

It wouldn't be until my divorce, when I moved into a tiny studio apartment in Manhattan, that my world views would be questioned. This time, it wouldn't be a slight, blue-eyed, curly-haired Jewish man from Alaska that would push back against my perspective. Instead, it would be a tiny Saint Lucian woman named Sabina.

Sabina is a Bronx-born, Saint Lucian-raised Caribbean woman who stands about 5 feet 2 inches tall. When I first met her, she had a head full of tightly curled hair that was typically pushed away from her forehead by an elastic headband, so that her hair stood up in a halo around her head. She had a large, beautiful mouth and eyes framed by delicate lashes. Her pretty face often misled people into thinking she was a soft woman, a gentle woman. Which, to some degree, she was. She had a big, loving heart and a nurturing soul. But life had been hard and unforgiving, and she kept much of herself guarded.

Her life had been shadowed by abuse and discrimination, and her cynicism warred with her inherent gentleness.

I met Sabina at my first job after graduate school, and she took me under her wing the day I walked into our broken-down office.

She was the first Black person I regularly interacted with, and she quickly became one of my best friends. I sometimes wonder what my life would have been like if I hadn't met Sabina.

She saw my heart and the potential for love within it, and she nurtured it. She opened my eyes to a world I'd never seen before: the world outside of my tiny, isolated Punjabi bubble.

During our lunch breaks, we would walk through Central Park, arm in arm, sharing secrets and stories from our lives. Over the first few months of our friendship, I told her about Ravi, about my own prejudice, and about all the stereotypes and narratives about Black people I believed growing up. I shared how little I truly knew about the Black community.

I felt tremendous guilt and shame, feeling such intense love for my Black friend, knowing the terrible thoughts and conversations about the Black community I'd participated in for so many years.

She told me to use my shame to fuel my desire to learn more about the world around me. Instead of wasting time with guilt, she advised, "Spend your time learning."

I would ask her questions that, to others, would seem offensive. And she would give brutally honest answers. She never, not once, became upset with me for asking her my most invasive questions, and she pushed me to ask more.

Why do Black women wear weaves and wigs? At what age is it okay to allow your Black child to get a weave or braids or whatever hairstyle he/she wants? Why don't you like being called African American? Why does that person prefer being called African American, but that person prefers to identify as Black? Is Caribbean American the correct term for you? Why are you okay with that person using certain words but not okay with that other person using them?

An educator at heart, Sabina encouraged me to challenge myself, to ask questions others were afraid to ask.

"How can I expect you to learn if I'm not willing to share what I know when you ask me?" she once said, when I asked her if it was problematic that I relied so heavily on her to educate myself on Black culture. "The internet and books can only teach you so much. You need to do the work of reading and researching, but I'm here for when you have questions."

One day, after coming back from visiting the nurses' station (we worked in a long-term care facility), I was pondering over some of the remarks the head nurse had made about struggling with not having money to cover some of her expenses.

"Why do Black women spend so much money on weaves and getting their nails done, and then complain about not having money?" I asked Sabina. As a woman who never spent much money on herself, I was new to the concept of self-care. I also had a strong judgmental streak and found myself judging the head nurse for her choices.

"First of all, it's ignorant and prejudiced as fuck to suggest that only Black women spend money on looking good. That's not a Black thing. That's a people thing," Sabina corrected me, her Saint Lucian accent thick. Whenever she spent time in the kitchen downstairs, she'd come back to the office with a thicker accent. She had a couple of friends working the food lines who were from Saint Lucia, and I loved hearing them talk to each other. I didn't realize the nuances in the accents of people from each Caribbean island.

"But regardless, we've been told our whole lives we aren't good-looking or good enough," Sabina explained. "And so now we take pride in our looks. We want to feel beautiful because for so long we were told we weren't. But also, everyone has the right to do what makes them feel good about themselves. It doesn't matter if money is tight, you need to feel good about yourself."

"Why do you get so upset if someone calls you African American?" I asked another time. "And why do some Black people get offended if you call them Black? It's a little confusing."

"I am not African," she said firmly. "I am Caribbean. I am from the Caribbean, and I am American. I am Caribbean American. I don't have any connection to my African roots; the white people took those away from us. So I am Caribbean in my blood. And people can decide what they like to be called. I like to be called Black. I am a Black woman. It is how I have lived in America."

From questions about income disparities to sexual stereotypes to hair textures, Sabina would listen to me, clicking her tongue ring against the back of her teeth, and answer all my questions during our long lunch break walks. She taught me to challenge myself when my old belief systems reared their ugly heads, when I made presumptions about a person because of the color of their skin. She showed me how to challenge my judgments and to explore how Black history has impacted the trajectory of the Black experience in America.

I worked in an area of Harlem heavily populated with people of African or Caribbean descent, and as a result many of the men I dated were the children of African or Caribbean immigrants. They spoke the language or dialect of their respective cultures, ate the foods from their cultures, and reminded me of everything I loved in my own upbringing: flavor, spice, color, vibrancy.

But they were also different from me. They didn't remind me of Ravi—and that was exactly what I needed. Men similar enough in cultural richness but disparate enough where I wouldn't see my ex in them.

After one particularly painful breakup, Sabina and I decided to take a trip together. One summer she took me home to Saint Lucia to meet her family, cooking me bake fish, baking homemade bread, and walking with me along the island as we picked mangos and bit into their hot, juicy flesh. She'd laugh at me as I tried untangling my long hair with fingers sticky with soursop. At night she'd teach me how to brush her kinky hair and teased me when I became frustrated after trying to detangle it.

"If you have a baby with a Black man, you better learn this, gyal," she advised, as she undid the tangles I created in her hair.

Sabina was one of my life's greatest loves, a friendship that saved me and opened up my heart and mind to the realities of my own ignorance and prejudice. And on some days, when I reflect on my life, I see her as my salvation.

Sabina was not only my first Black friend but she was also one of the most intelligent, hard-working, and loving humans I'd ever met in my life. She was the antagonist to the character of the *kahla bhanda* (Black person) I had in my head my entire life.

The end of my friendship with Sabina is one of the more painful parts of my self-discovery journey. We fought shortly before I left New York City, and in my youthful pettiness and pride, I moved to California without saying a proper goodbye to her. Though I reached out to her multiple times after my move, the damage my petty pride inflicted on our friendship was too great to undo.

It still creates an ache in my belly when I think of her, particularly because it was her coaching and guidance that allowed me to keep my heart open to a man who would quickly become the greatest love of my life: Mel.

Meeting Mel

Shortly after I moved home to California, I met a white man. I thought briefly that we had potential for a long-term relationship. But I felt loud when I was with him, too colorful and too textured. I felt different. I felt like "the other." And when he used the word "exotic" to describe me, I knew it wouldn't work. I began dating men from different racial and ethnic backgrounds until one day I decided I wanted to explore dating Indian men again. I so terribly missed speaking my language with my partner. I missed dancing to *bhangra*, making *achaar* for our dinners, and cooking the foods of my cultural roots.

The first Indian person I dated after my divorce was a Hindu Punjabi man. On our second date, he asked me what types of relationships I'd been in and if they'd been with people outside of our culture. When I told him about the two meaningful relationships I'd had with Ghanaian men, he put down his drink. "You've been with *kahle*?" he asked. "You've let *kahle* inside of you?"

I stared at him for a moment, tilted my head, and responded, "Yes. And they treated me better than you clearly would be able to." And I got up and left, walking out of the restaurant while I blocked his number on my phone.

The second Indian man cracked a joke about penis sizes when he learned about my dating history, and the third made it overtly clear that he was "okay with" the fact I'd dated African men (as if I'd needed his permission or approval).

Tired of the disappointment, I decided to step back from dating, unsure if I would ever find a partner suited to me.

Weeks before I decided to take a break from the dating scene in Los Angeles, Mel and I had connected on a dating app. When we connected online, we exchanged numbers and messaged each other briefly, but our schedules were chaotic. He explained he needed a few weeks for his schedule to stabilize before we could meet.

I wrote him off, thinking he was one of those men who wanted to text but never meet up. To my surprise, he texted me a day after I deleted all my dating apps. I told him I wasn't interested in dating anyone for a few months, and he asked if he could call me and see if I still wanted to take a break from dating after speaking with him. I agreed to the phone call, and as soon as I heard his voice, my curiosity spiked.

His voice was low, rich, and deep. It was filled with life and humor.

"Can I get one shot at taking you out?" he asked during our brief call. "I can make reservations for us at a great brunch spot if you're open to it this weekend. No pressure at all. I was sincerely busy these past few weeks, but I'm very interested in meeting you." He was so sweet and easy to talk to on the phone that I found myself nodding and agreeing to his request.

That weekend, I met Mel for the first time. He was the most amazing man I'd ever encountered, and he is the only man I've been with since my eyes first met his. I still remember the grin that broke out across his face when he first saw me, the way his eyes quickly roved over me to see if I was indeed the person he'd matched with on Bumble. My heart rate increased, and within five minutes of sitting next to him, absorbing the quickness of his laugh and the flash of mischief on his face when he cracked a joke, I knew my life was going to change.

Our romance was fast and intense. Within a handful of months we were living together. Because he is considerably older than me, Mel knew what he was looking for in a partner when he met me. He made his hopes clear from the beginning. "No games," he told me. "When I joined those dating apps, I was looking for partnership. You're what I want in a life partner. I've lived a lot of life. I know what I want, and you're it."

Though he wooed me with fancy restaurants and sweet words, it was his kindness and thoughtfulness that kept me hooked. He remembered little details about me, the foods I liked, the things I was interested in learning more about. After we'd been together for about a year, we'd both noticed my mood had changed. I was struggling with depression and anxiety (which I've battled since my youth), and though I had returned to therapy, I still felt a heavy loneliness and sadness throughout my days.

One evening, he came home with chamomile and lavender flowers as well as an aromatherapy kit. He placed them on the kitchen table, next to a box of chocolate eclairs he'd picked up from my favorite bakery. "The lady at Whole Foods said these flowers and the essential oils will help with your anxiety. And I thought the eclairs would be a tasty treat for you. I want to help you get through this, but I don't know what I'm supposed to do," he said, wrapping his arms around me from behind as I buried my face in the lavender, breathing in the calming scent. He nuzzled me from behind and whispered, "I just want you to be happy. Tell me what I need to do to help you."

Mel was the first man who treated me as a complete equal while simultaneously making me feel protected and cherished. He was the first man who encouraged me to speak my mind without filtering myself, the first man who made me feel like he truly saw me.

He was also the first man I'd dated who called himself "Black." He is not African. Some people would call him African American, but he prefers to be called Black.

"None of this PC, 'African American' bullshit," he once said. "Say it like it is. I'm Black."

Mel does not speak a different language. Born in Virginia, he grew up with Southern cooking as part of his cultural heritage, and he does not own any non-Western garb. When we first met, he listened exclusively to hip-hop or R & B music, cracked jokes using racial slurs, and called me his Punjabi Queen. As we've grown together, things have evolved (he's cut back on the racially charged jokes and expanded his music selection), but the core of who he is remains unchanged.

He pushes me to ask daring questions about race and color. He challenges me to be uncomfortable as I seek to improve and grow as a person. He is secure, unafraid, and unapologetic. And he encourages me to be the same.

He listens to me with patience. When we argue, he steps back to see my perspective. He randomly buys me flowers because he knows they make me smile. He allows himself to be vulnerable and seeks to improve his emotional intelligence on a daily basis. He awkwardly attempts to say words in my language, grinning when his tongue stumbles over itself. He is the first man to encourage me to be unabashedly myself. And he accepts me.

So, does it matter that he cannot speak my language? That he is not Sikh? That his skin tone is shades darker than my own? That my parents, who accept and support my relationship with him, cannot connect with him over Punjabi culture?

I used to think these things would matter. And even now, I sometimes think about how our child will never truly know what it is like to grow up in a fully Punjabi household. Or, on the flip side, a fully Black household. I worry about their sense of identity, of the rejection they may face from either of our communities.

We talk about it, this potential dilution of both of our cultures as we navigate raising a biracial and bicultural child together. He finds the challenge thrilling, energized by providing our child a door to two different worlds. It is our responsibility, he says, to give our child a strong sense of identity. We can see our child's mixed race as a dilution of two cultures or we can see it as a union of two cultures. It is our choice.

He has complete and utter faith that our child will grow up with nothing but love and acceptance, that the outside world will not impact the unassailable sense of self-love and self-value we will nurture within our child. His unfettered confidence and faith in this vision almost drowns out my own fears, which are in no small part fueled by my knowledge of my own history of prejudice.

"All we can do is love and protect our baby. The world is going to do what the world is going to do. We'll just need to teach our child to thrive in whatever world we live in," Mel said to me when I asked him if he worried that people from our respective communities wouldn't fully accept our child. He placed his hand over my growing belly and kissed my cheek. "Everything will be okay."

I don't know what the future holds. I don't know what kind of person our child will be, or whether they will struggle with their sense of identity in the same ways I did.

What I do know is that Mel has been my reckoning, the underlying current that pushes me every day to fight to be my best self. He is an amazing father and an unshakeable support system to both me and our child.

And the reality is I never would have found him if I hadn't cleared my eyes from the prejudice raging through my South Asian community—and I never would have challenged my own anti-Black prejudice if I hadn't learned so much from Sabina. These two individuals changed me forever, dual catalysts who ushered me into an irrevocable personal evolution.

Part 2

CHAPTER 5

The Model Minority Myth is a Racial Wedge

—

As you read this chapter, please keep in mind that I will be referring often to Asian Americans as a group broadly, and I include myself and the South Asian community in that broad group. The model minority myth does not differentiate between the different Asian countries, communities, or cultures. For this reason, my personal use of the word "we" in this chapter (as well as the subsequent chapter) when referring to the Asian American experience is intentional.

I sometimes wonder what would have happened if Ravi's roommate, Joshua, had challenged me again the day after our argument, when I apologized to him for my outburst regarding *The Vagina Monologues*. If he'd caught onto my language and realized I was more concerned about what he thought of me than about learning from our conversation. I wonder what would have happened if my "whataboutmeism" had been called out by someone.

Years later, during the summer of 2020, I learned that my beliefs about the American Dream were the by-products of the "model minority" myth.

It was this myth and the myopia of my "what-about-me" mentality that was at the root of how I perceived the Black experience in America. I learned that, despite what I believed, my experiences with racism were not comparable to that of the Black community's experience with anti-Blackness. I lived in this country as a "model minority," at once suffocated by the label and the expectations arising from it but simultaneously reaping the benefits of its political and social positioning.

What is the Model Minority Myth?

The Asian American community, which encompasses people from all the countries in Asia, is positioned as a demographic that is hardworking, diligent, disciplined, and respectful, all qualities that have allegedly allowed us to enjoy a higher degree of socioeconomic and educational success than our Black counterparts.

The reality is that, despite what my family led me to believe, the advances the Asian community made in America in the twentieth century were not exclusively the by-products of hard work and diligence alone. They were the result of immigration policies that prioritized skilled and educated workers from Asian countries.

Historically, the United States government heavily restricted Asian immigration through racist policies, like the Chinese Exclusion Act, and organizations, like the Asiatic Exclusion League (which was formed for the sole purpose of lobbying against the immigration of Asians into America) (The Pluralism Project 2020).

Many of the Asian immigrants from China, Japan, Korea, the Philippines, and India in the late 1800s and early 1900s were physical laborers. The contribution these Asian immigrants made to the American workforce was a source of agitation and frustration for many Americans, who blamed these immigrants for taking away or "stealing" jobs from white people.

In 1917, a law was passed to prevent people from Asia from entering the United States, though this law didn't cover people from Japan, since policies against Japanese immigration already existed. The law also didn't apply to the Philippines because it was a U.S. territory at the time. However, in 1924, the policy was modified to exclude *all* immigrants from Asia (The Pluralism Project 2020).

Over the next handful of decades, the government modified their anti-Asian exclusionary policies, and in 1965 passed the 1965 Immigration Act. This policy allowed Asian immigration to America, albeit under two conditions: Asian immigrants had to be "skilled," or they had to have family already residing in the United States. There were annual quotas for immigrants from each Asian country, but there were exceptions. Nonquota immigrants included students and "intellectuals," military brides from Asia, and war orphans adopted by American families (Wu 2015).

The Immigration Act of 1965 plays a critical role in the Asian American experience even today. As the country overhauled its immigration laws, policy makers determined that immigrants should be selected based on their potential to contribute to the U.S. economy and their ability to create whole families through reunification of family members (Pew

Research 2015). This law operated upon a preference-based system that gave priority to relatives of U.S. citizens, refugees, professionals, and individuals with specialized skills—blatantly favoring highly educated immigrants.

What resulted was a wave of immigration that brought in people with credentials, education, and training—traits that confirmed ideologies already taking root about Asian Americans being the "model minority" in America.

My own grandfather came to this country on the heels of his engineering degree. For so much of my life, I touted my family's success and opportunity to the resilience, tenacity, and hard work displayed by my grandparents and father. Though they may indeed have demonstrated these characteristics, the reality is that when they came to this country, they already had an advantage over the members of the Black community. My grandfather was allowed into this country explicitly because the government expected him to contribute to the country's economy as an engineer.

In her book *The Color of Success: Asian Americans and the Origins of the Model Minority*, historian and Professor Ellen Wu explains that Asian minorities in the U.S. actively tried to assimilate into American culture. They portrayed themselves as law-abiding, upstanding citizens who could integrate seamlessly into America, produce obedient children, and uphold traditional family values (Wu 2015).

When I studied Professor Wu's research for this book, so many elements from my upbringing were brought into focus. I was always told to be a "good girl," to maintain my family's honor, to be obedient, and to get a good education. As a community, my family members and fellow South Asians fed into this model minority trope without even being consciously aware of it.

It wasn't until researching for this book that I began to understand *why* my community and the broader Asian community fed into this myth. Given the history of Asian exclusion and anti-Asian antagonism, living up to the "model minority" trope offered us a blanket of protection, a way for us to separate ourselves from the targeted anti-Black racism white America displayed toward Black Americans.

After the Immigration Act of 1965, America cast the Asian population in America as people who had assimilated. Asians were perceived by American society as politically nonthreatening counterparts to the politically active Black community (Wu 2016).

The media positioned Asian success as the by-product of Asian obedience to government, suggesting that *complying* with the state rather than fighting against it was the recipe for success. According to the media, being "good Americans" was the key reason why Asian communities were more successful than the Black community. By promoting stories of successful Asians, the government and media attempted to weaken the Black civil rights movement.

It's critical to note that the media heavily celebrated stories of successful Asians during the era of the civil rights movement, but stories of struggling Asian communities were essentially hidden from public consumption (Wu 2015).

So how is all this relevant to a conversation about anti-Blackness in South Asian communities? Our parents and grandparents were literally brought here because of their advanced qualifications and skills, specifically preselected for success.

It's no wonder our earning potential and our acceptance by American society would be so much higher than our Black counterparts. And reaping the socioeconomic and political rewards of our positioning within American society, it's no wonder why, as a collective community, we have a tendency to feed into the myth centered around us.

How the Model Minority Myth was Racially Divisive

Essentially, the "model minority" trope was intentionally constructed to pit the Asian American community (with their "hard-earned" success despite their hardships) against the Black community (whose suffering apparently resulted from their lack of determination to work hard).

In the 1960s, when the immigration policies in America changed, the model minority stereotype was socially weaponized against the Black community. Stories of Asian success in America were used as "proof" that there was equal opportunity for all minority communities (including the Black community) to also find success (Wu 2015).

For example, the Japanese American experience was reframed as a "rags to riches" story, strengthening the message that hard work and discipline were enough to pull an entire ethnic population out of the trenches. In 1966, an article titled "Success Story, Japanese-American Style" was published in the *New York Times*. The author of the piece, William Pettersen, states: For all the well-meaning programs and countless scholarly studies now focused on the Negro, we barely know how to repair the damage that the slave traders started. The history of Japanese Americans, however, challenges every such generalization about ethnic minorities [...]. Barely more than twenty years after the end of the wartime camps, this is a minority that has risen above even prejudiced criticism. [...] Every attempt to hamper their progress resulted only in enhancing their determination to succeed (Pettersen 1966).

This 1966 article basically fed a narrative to the American people that the Japanese community in America not only survived wartime camps but also thrived in society despite the history of prejudice and oppression they faced.

Later that year, *The US News & World Report* published a piece titled "Success Story of One Minority Group in the US," which focused on Chinese Americans. It stated, "At a time when it is being proposed that hundreds of billions be spent on uplifting Negroes and other minorities, the nation's 300,000 Chinese Americans are moving ahead on their own with no help from anyone else" (US News & World Report 1966).

The media began elevating stories of Asian subgroups and spotlighting them as examples of fortitude and resilience, pitting these success stories against the plights experienced by the Black community. Socioeconomic disadvantages and struggles were, according to these success stories, not the by-product of policy, government, or social structure but were the consequences of lack of determination and hard work.

By promoting these stories of "model minorities," it became easier for the government to deny the demands of the Black community. The myth allowed people to ask: If one marginalized community was able to figure it out, why couldn't the Black community?

I had ingrained this very narrative into my understanding of the world. I had become, without being aware of it, a megaphone for the model minority myth. Wasn't that my argument to Joshua, all those years ago in the basement kitchen of Ravi's apartment? That my father had worked tirelessly to give me a good life, and Black people just needed to work harder?

The racial wedge created by the model minority myth was widened with the release of a report written by President Lyndon Johnson's assistant secretary of labor, Daniel Patrick Moynihan.

In 1965, Moynihan published the "The Negro Family: The Case for National Action" (also known as the Moynihan Report). In his report, Moynihan discussed the resonating consequences of slavery on the Black community as well the inequalities and inequities the Black community struggled with post-Reconstruction. Though history unquestionably played a role in the Black community's contemporary plight, Moynihan argued that the poverty observed in the Black community was also the result of the Black community's dysfunctional family structures (Office of Policy Planning and Research 1965).

Though the report acknowledged that Black people experienced life in America as a marginalized group, with fewer opportunities than their white counterparts, it also decried the structure of Black families (which were widely single-parent families headed by females). Though Moynihan did call for government support to improve the economic prospects of Black families, he suggested it would truly only be through rehabilitation within the community itself (and not through social programs or policy) that the Black community could see lasting change.

Moynihan's report was groundbreaking in that it acknowledged outright that American history had disadvantaged Black Americans and urged the government to provide jobs and economic support to the Black community. The controversy in the report, however, lay in it also positioning those who struggled in poverty as personally responsible for their own fates (Geary 2015).

The messaging promoted during this time period served to enhance the dichotomy between Asian and Black communities in America, elevating the former as a group to be applauded for its hard work, tenacity, and assimilation and denigrating the latter as a group incapable of the discipline required for socioeconomic improvement.

A half a century later, this myth is very much a fabric of the racial landscape of American society.

The subject of assimilation came up during a conversation with a friend named Riz, who immigrated to America from Bangladesh with her family when she was ten. Riz shared her experience of coming to America and naturally falling into the rhythm of becoming the "model" minority.

"For immigrants who come into this country, who are trying to feed into the American Dream, we were taught that the best way to feed into the American Dream was to assimilate and to become more like those who are white," Riz explained. "And that was essentially what my parents were doing. They were learning how to speak English better, they were trying to feed into this culture and took a stance of 'we obey authority, we pursue education, we assimilate into this white culture.'"

Hazeem, a Pakistani man who moved to America with his family when he was in elementary school, explained how his family also engaged with this concept of a "model minority."

"I noticed my parents would highlight the Asian students who fit that role of being a model minority, but they would just ignore the ones who didn't," Hazeem told me.

"The Asian kids whose grades maybe weren't as good or who listened to rap music were discounted. And then with other races, it was the opposite. They would focus more on the students who represented the more racist stereotypes of being gang members or doing drugs, and they'd focus on the Black and Hispanic kids who were doing those things versus the students from those same racial groups who were doing really, really well. Like, if someone they knew who was Black or Hispanic was doing well, it was almost as if they were able to do it *despite* their race. So we kind of fed into the model minority myth in that way."

The Pressure of "Being Successful"

Growing up, there was an intense emphasis in my family on the criticality of education as the foundation for financial and social success. Ironically, neither of my parents have college educations, but the financial success resulting from being business owners was a suitable way to nullify their lack of formal education.

Essentially, if a person has not yet achieved financial success, then education was a measuring stick by which to judge a person's value in my community. Additionally, there was (and continues to be) a belief in South Asian culture that education and job security are *not* "givens" within the Black community the way they are in the South Asian community.

For instance, a few years after my divorce, I reconnected with a relative who lived in New York and is a Hindu Punjabi woman. I had distanced myself from many people in my community after my divorce and was slowly reconnecting with old family friends and relatives. During our conversation, I told this relative about Mel.

Almost immediately, she said, "Oh, wow! He is Black? Does he have a job?"

My eyes rolled in frustration, even though I had anticipated her reaction.

I responded calmly, despite my irritation. "He doesn't have a job. He has his own business."

"Is it a successful business? What is his business?" she asked.

After explaining to her what Mel actually did for a living, I was then asked, "Is he educated?"

Given I'd already told her Mel was in his late thirties and had an established business, his education status wasn't something that would be particularly relevant in our conversation. But her ingrained beliefs about Black people were that they did not tend to have college degrees.

She did not ask me what he was like, what his personality was like, how we met, or why I loved him. Her first two (and primary) concerns were (1) is he employed and (2) is he educated.

Years earlier, when she'd first learned of Ravi (my boyfriend turned husband turned ex-husband), the questions were, "Do you like his family? How did you meet? Do you get along with his mother?" The glaring differences in how she received news of both these men are unquestionably the result of their racial differences.

A similar conversation occurred between me and an Indian colleague I met at orientation when I started a new job shortly after meeting Mel. A young therapist-in-training from New Delhi, she asked me, "Does your boyfriend have a degree? Your parents are okay with you dating him, even though he is Black? Do they know about him?"

At the time, I didn't realize how problematic these questions were because I expected them (which was problematic in itself). Questions like these are the by-products of the divisiveness created by the myth of the model minority. Those who have fed into the myth feel discomfort and surprise when people cross the divide to engage in relationships with each other. The seamless way these questions are integrated into our conversations are also examples of how, by buying into the model minority myth, we are active participants in an inherently racist social hierarchy.

The truth is, though, that just as this myth harms Black people, it also harms the very people who attempt to live up to it.

CHAPTER 6

The Toll of the Model Minority Myth on Asians

Though the myth of the model minority harmed the Black community and continues to create a divide between the Black and Asian communities, it's important to note that this myth is also harmful to the Asian community itself.

The myth overlooks the history of Asian presence in America and the reality that the government viewed Asian immigrants as threats to the American workforce. Asian immigrants were perceived to be so foreign that they were legally barred from becoming full citizens.

The myth of the model minority also treats Asian Americans as a monolith, discounting the diversity of Asian countries represented by the Asian American population. In fact, the twenty-two million Asian Americans who comprise the Asian diaspora in America can trace their lineage to over twenty different countries from the Indian subcontinent, East Asia, and Southeast Asia. Each of these countries has their own unique histories, languages, cultures, and customs (Budiman and Ruiz 2021).

By clumping all Asians together as a "model minority," the myth erases the distinct and unique identities of each Asian culture within the Asian diaspora. Even within the South Asian community itself, and within the Indian community more specifically, there are nuances and differences between individuals from different South Asian countries as well as from different parts of India.

What's more, the pressures placed upon Asian youth to uphold the status of a "model minority" are exhausting and even dangerous.

Research shows that Asian American and Pacific Islanders have the highest rate of death by suicide in females between the ages of fifteen and twenty-four in the U.S. Male Asian Americans and Pacific Islanders in the same age range have the second-highest rate of suicide deaths in the U.S. compared to any other racial or ethnic group, second only to white males (Lee et al. 2009).

Overall, Asian Americans suffer from higher rates of suicide, anxiety, and depression than any other racial or ethnic group in America. Researchers from a study examining mental health amongst Asian American youth suggest expectations of societal status and financial success play a large part in the degradation of mental health within Asian American youth (Lee et al. 2009).

Asian American participants in the study agreed that their parents set high expectations for academic and professional success. These study participants expressed that the "Asian American stereotype" of being smart and professionally successful impacted their mental health, and it also impacted what they studied in college and graduate school (Lee et al. 2009).

Another key contributor to the mental health struggle of Asian American youth is the family structures prevalent in

Asian American culture. Asian cultural values often place an emphasis on family obligation. It is not uncommon to see Asian youth care for their parents as they age. First- and second-generation Asian Americans may still operate as their parents' or grandparents' interpreters or translators and often provide assistance with transportation and caretaking (Lee et al. 2009).

When I read this research, the realities of the pressure and expectations of the model minority myth resonated with me. I vividly recalled the innumerable times I curled up on my bed or on the floor, shaking with anxiety as large exams loomed ahead of me. Most of my friends in high school were Asian (Korean, Cambodian, Vietnamese, Indian, and Chinese), and we quietly competed to get the highest grades, the best SAT scores, and the most impressive college acceptance letters. We held deep respect for our parents and built our lives around being obedient children.

Despite being a deep lover of literature and creative writing and having little affinity for math or science, I made a promise to my grandfather to become a doctor. I matriculated as a student at UCLA with a premed concentration. I lost chunks of hair my first quarter at UCLA, losing sleep over poor chemistry grades and my inability to pay attention to my science professors droning on and on about content I didn't care about. I struggled with suicidal ideations and eating disorders, scaring my mother with the depth of my unhappiness and depression. I still remember her voice when my roommate called her from the hospital after I passed out as I climbed out of my bunk bed, operating on little food and too much caffeine. I'd fallen to the ground and bruised the bones in my foot, my blood pressure elevated and heart racing.

But I flourished in my literature classes, going to coffeehouses as soon as they opened to curl up with my copy of *Northanger Abbey* and write fictional accounts of nonfictional college life experiences. By the end of my first year of college, I'd dropped my premed concentration and switched to English literature, accepting the vague sense of "I let them down" that followed me around my college campus for the remaining three years.

Throughout middle school, high school, and college, I made myself sick and miserable trying to keep up with the "good girl" persona I knew brought my parents so much pride. This pressure to be the "good girl" kept me "in my place" during college. It is what propelled me to marry Ravi and played a huge role in my development

My entire life—up until age twenty-seven, when I left my marriage and met Sabina—I fed into the model minority myth.

I wasn't alone. My friend Mark, a man of Korean descent who grew up in Los Angeles and was raised by Korean immigrant parents, shared his family's experience of learning about the Virginia Tech shootings in 2007.

"My mom and I had the same reaction when we saw the story developing on the news," Mark told me during a conversation about the model minority myth.

"We were both thinking, 'Please don't be Korean, please don't be Korean.' And it turned out that the shooter was a Korean guy. And when that news broke, both of us were like 'Fuck. This makes us look bad.' But that was our initial thought, which is really messed up if you think about it."

He continued, "The initial thought should be 'What a tragedy. What can we do to support the family? What can we do to make sure this never happens again?' But I kept thinking 'Please don't be Korean' because if the shooter was Korean, that meant my life would become harder. Now the jokes that people aimed at me would be Virginia Tech jokes. That's more ammo for people to stereotype me because I am Korean. And that was a problem for me growing up. It was like, 'Don't be a problem kid because it'll make Koreans look bad.' To the point where it's like 'Don't be a mass shooter, because it'll make Koreans look bad.'"

Mark and I had exchanged stories about our experiences growing up in our respective communities, and despite our families coming from different countries in Asia and him being a man and I a woman, we both found strong similarities with regards to our feelings about our "otherness" and the need to assimilate into "whiteness."

"I had one teacher in high school who grew up when Bruce Lee had hit his peak in popularity," Mark shared. "There was apparently a lot of Asian people in pop culture during that time because of kung fu and karate. My teacher said something about how, when she was younger, it was like people wanted to be Asian because of how popular these kinds of movies were. And one of my classmates yelled out, 'Why in the world would you want to be *Asian?*' and everyone laughed. I remember I made myself laugh too. It's pretty sad to look back on that. It was a joke to be Asian. It wasn't something to strive for. Kung fu and karate were cool, but you would never want to actually be Asian. That experience further reinforced the idea of 'yeah, I want to be white.'"

Mark also pointed out, "I was in college when I first found out about this model minority concept. It felt weird because my professor was placing Koreans toward the top, as part of the model minority group. Growing up, my family was low income. We didn't have a lot of money at all. We're not wealthy by any means. So I never even felt part of the model minority in that way. But that's what was projected on to me my whole life because I'm, you know, East Asian. So, you know, I should be successful because so many other East Asians are successful."

Mark spoke to yet another reason why the model minority myth is harmful to Asian communities: it nullifies the challenges experienced by individual members of the Asian community. By suggesting that Asian Americans are a homogenous, monolithic group, this myth neglects the vast differences in income between different groups of Asians. In fact, income disparities amongst Asians in the U.S. are the greatest of any racial group in America (Allard 2011).

Government data show that while Asian Americans are ranked as having the highest earnings of any racial or ethnic group in the U.S., the gap in income between the highest earners and the lowest earners is huge. In 2016, Asian Americans at the top of the income ladder made 8.7 times as much income as those toward the bottom of the income ladder (which means that while some Asian Americans at the top of the ladder could make $113,000 per year, those at the bottom could make as little as $13,000 per year) (Pew Research 2018).

The model minority myth discounts these steep income disparities, ignoring the challenges and struggles with which millions of Asians in America must contend.

What's more, even education, one of the hallmarks for success according to the model minority myth, is varied in the Asian American community. For instance, 75 percent of Indian Americans have at least a bachelor's degree, while 20 percent of Vietnamese Americans have less than a high school diploma. Over two-thirds of Indian Americans are in professional jobs (including management), while 20 percent of Vietnamese Americans hold low-paying service jobs (US Bureau of Labor Statistics 2011).

Essentially, while many Asians reap the benefits of immigration policies favoring skilled and educated immigrants, there are large groups of Asian immigrants (particularly refugees from Southeast Asia) who do not experience the degree of success promoted by the media.

Because this book focuses on the South Asian community specifically, and because I am speaking to my experiences as someone from the Indian community, it is important to highlight that not only do Indian Americans have the highest incomes of any other Asian group in America (and are actually, on average, one of the most affluent group of people in the country as a whole), we are also the most highly educated.

This level of success is in no small part due to the immigration policies that favored the immigration of skilled and educated workers from South Asia. My father achieved the American Dream because he worked hard. The realities of his struggle and his efforts are unquestionable. However, he also came here with a father who had an engineering degree. His cousins, aunts, uncles, and other family members all came to America because they had education and skill sets desired by the U.S. government, or because they were relatives of immigrants who had those privileges. They had community members who could help them assimilate, help them become citizens, and help them establish themselves in this new country.

It is this reality that I truly failed to comprehend and understand when I stood in that kitchen with Joshua all those years ago, arguing with him about racism and my thoughts on the American Dream. I had not yet accepted the reality of the inherent privilege woven into my family's immigration to America.

I never truly understood the distinction between the Indian and larger South Asian experience with racism and that of the Black experience. And I had no idea how I contributed so often to the myth of the model minority, to the racial divisiveness of the myth, when I said things like, "My family worked hard for what we have! My grandfather came here and had to build a life from scratch!"

I am not in any way discounting the reality that even within the subgroup of the South Asian and, more specifically, Indian community there exists income disparities and a struggle with racism and discrimination in America. I specifically address not only the ways the myth of the model minority has benefited the South Asian community but also the way it has burdened us because I want to ensure my readers know I am aware of the toll of this myth as well as the realities it ignores (particularly that education does not guarantee financial security).

At the same time (because two realities can coexist), as a whole, our community has never (and will never) truly understood the centuries-old impact of American slavery and the ensuing generational trauma and loss of opportunity experienced by Black Americans. We had the privilege of immigration policies that allowed our communities to experience opportunities not given to Black communities. We also benefited from the fight for civil rights carried forward by the Black community in a way that I never truly understood.

It took me years to understand that my experience with racism could not truly be compared to that of Black people in America.

Part 3

CHAPTER 7

The U.S. History I Didn't Know

———

My use of the term "anti-Blackness" throughout this book is intentional.

kihana miraya ross, a professor at Northwestern University who intentionally keeps her name in lowercase, wrote an opinion piece for the *New York Times*. In her op-ed titled "Call It What It Is: Anti-Blackness," ross explains why the term "anti-Blackness" is important to use when discussing the Black experience in America (versus simply using the word "racism").

She says, "To be clear, 'racism' isn't a meaningless term. But it's a catchall that can encapsulate anything from Black people being denied fair access to mortgage loans, to Asian students being burdened with a 'model minority' label. It's not specific" (ross 2020).

The reason it's important to "be specific" in conversations about anti-Blackness in America is because of America's history of dehumanizing and targeting Black people specifically.

Professor ross gives some more insight into America's historical treatment of Black people when she says, "Black people were rendered as property, built this country, spilled literal blood, sweat and tears into the soil from which we eat, the water we drink, and the air we breathe. The *thingification* of black people is a fundamental component of the identity of this nation" (ross 2020).

The "Thingification" of Black People

My knowledge of American history was the watered-down version offered by my conservative Catholic high school. I don't know if this is still the case in schools around the country, but I don't know of many people who had history courses that truly depicted the stark depravity inherent in this country's founding.

Of course, we learned about slavery. Enslaved people were property, to be bought, sold, gifted, or inherited by slave owners.

But the "thingification" of Black people, the actual brutality of chattel slavery itself, was glossed over. My history lessons didn't discuss enslaved children. *Children* wore iron shackles and toiled in merciless conditions. At any point, these children could be taken from their parents and sold into different families. Enslaved women were regularly raped by slave owners, and their children would be enslaved. The hair of enslaved people was used in furniture (Flood 2021), and their teeth were pulled to make dentures for white people (even George Washington's dentures included teeth from enslaved people) (Wills 2020).

In fact, in the process of writing this book, I even learned that the term "slave" was meant to "thingify" Black people, which is why academics in some circles are now encouraging the use of the term "enslaved people" to remind us slaves were just that: actual people (Waldman 2015).

My school followed the basic curricula of most high schools: use the textbook as a road map, give assignments, and hope your students actually learn something.

Everything was so vague. We skimmed over so much. We were often taught to memorize and recite the Gettysburg Address. We learned the North fought the South, the South were the "bad guys," and Abraham Lincoln freed all the enslaved people. The textbook chapter would end, and we'd move onto another chapter about the American Revolution.

As students, my classmates and I would cram for our tests to get the A's we needed to get into good colleges. We weren't learning to *learn*. We were learning to keep up with college admissions requirements.

I remember learning about the abolition of slavery, and I remember learning about Reconstruction. But I don't recall diving into the fact that abolishing slavery didn't in any way actually humanize the freed enslaved people. In fact, the era that followed (Reconstruction) ushered in a period in American history when white America built into its foundation an institutionalized racial hierarchy that has not, to this day, been fully dismantled.

What's more, the word "lynching," which is one of the vilest manifestations of the thingification of Black people, was barely used in my American history classes.

I didn't know that over 4,500 Black people were lynched between 1882 and 1962 in America, and this number doesn't include other acts of violence against Black people during this time and doesn't account for any lynchings that remain unreported. In my history classes, we definitely didn't talk about lynchings happening as recently as the twentieth century (Equal Justice Initiative 2017).

And I don't remember learning that the lynching of Black people was considered a form of entertainment for Southern Americans. People would gather and cheer, setting up picnics to watch Black people be tortured and killed. Victims would be burned alive, dismembered alive, and even castrated alive. Their body parts, ashes, clothes, and even sexual organs would be sold to spectators to save as souvenirs of the "event" (Equal Justice Initiative 2017).

Some of these events would be quick, but others would be longer, drawn-out events that included food, speeches, and celebrating families. Newspaper articles would mention victims whose eyes were gouged out and whose ears were cut off, sometimes even referring to them as "Negro barbecues" (Dray 2002).

If reading about these lynchings makes you uncomfortable, I ask you to sit in that discomfort, because, as a community, we can't turn our eyes away from truth just because it's uncomfortable. Looking away doesn't mean the truths no longer exist, it just means we are engaging in willful ignorance, which is nothing short of tacit consent to the status quo.

And the truth is that for a sizable chunk of our nation's existence, American history so thoroughly dehumanized Black people that their mutilation and death was a source of fun, celebration, and sport for white Americans. Even after slavery ended, white America still treated Black people as if they held less value than animals, and the white people who brutalized Black people faced few (if any) repercussions from law enforcement.

A mere twelve years after slavery ended, Presidential Reconstruction led to laws known as "black codes." Black codes were created to restrict newly freed Black people and ensure they would still provide a cheap labor force to the South. These laws were a way to make white people in the South feel better about slavery ending and the law no longer openly sanctioning treating Black people like chattel (Equal Justice Initiative 2020).

Learning about the black codes was eye-opening. My knowledge of U.S. history suggested that the Black experience improved once slavery was abolished. The enslaved people were finally free, right? So things must have gotten so much better for Black people. Slavery was over, there was nowhere to go but up. As I educated myself more, I realized Black people had been freed from one type of brutal hell, had a brief and tumultuous respite during Reconstruction, and fell right back into another layer of hell. I felt overwhelmed by my own ignorance.

One night after reading about Presidential Reconstruction, I desperately needed to take the night off from writing.

I snuggled into Mel that night, tired from a long day of work and the fatigue that came from being hugely pregnant. My belly was almost the size of a large watermelon, but we'd figured out a way to cuddle on the sofa that didn't lead to one of us falling off.

It was raining outside, and the Christmas lights brought an air of cozy festivity to our home.

"Do you get depressed watching these documentaries?" I'd asked him. We had just watched 13th, a Netflix documentary on the racial inequities in America, with a focus on the prison system. The movie had made me cry (at that time most things made me cry, as I was thirty-six weeks pregnant).

"No," he said, playing with my hair. "I still learn something new whenever I watch these things, but I can't let myself get depressed every time I watch something about how Black people have been pushed down."

I thought about what he said. "How are you so strong?" I asked. "I feel like nothing fazes you, but I don't know if it's because you hide it or because you truly aren't fazed. I'm so sensitive, and you're the complete opposite. How can I be like you?"

"It's probably a little bit of both, I guess," he replied. "You know I compartmentalize things. But also, none of this is really new to me. I may not know the statistics, but I've lived the reality. I mean, Jesus Christ, my dad was alive during a time when he couldn't walk into a building because of the color of his skin. Watching a documentary about that isn't going to upset me. Black resilience is a survival mechanism. If I walked around getting fazed by every little damn thing, I'd get nothing done."

He kissed my hair. "And you don't need to be like me, babe. I love you because you're you."

Later that night, I thought about what he said about Black resilience, and I realized "resilient" was one of the most perfect words that could be used to describe Mel. And I began to see that this concept of "Black resilience" was a common theme in the research I was doing to learn more about Black history.

The next morning I read about black codes, and a rush of shame at my ignorance washed over me. My research showed me I really didn't know much about what Black people endured after slavery, even though this information has been available to me online for years. I had simply chosen not to pursue educating myself on it. I had judged an entire community of people and knew so little about their history in this country.

For example, when enslaved people were "freed," they were required to sign annual labor contracts to prove they were employed for the year. If they refused to sign these contracts, they would be arrested, fined, and forced into *unpaid* manual labor (they were essentially re-enslaved) (Equal Justice Initiative 2020).

Essentially, even after slavery was abolished in 1865, Black America continued to be oppressed, vilified, silenced, and controlled via these black codes.

Despite the innumerable barriers, the Black community consistently demonstrated resilience. After slavery was abolished and Reconstruction began, for the first time in American history, Black people ran for office, Black children went to school, and the Black community became politically active.

Unfortunately, this period was incredibly short lived.

Jim Crow—"Slavery by Another Name"

The end of Reconstruction in 1877 ushered in over a century of oppression under the Jim Crow laws, which would legalize the segregation of Black and white people. The black codes had laid a foundation for the continued and systematic oppression of Black people post-abolition, and the Jim Crow laws built upon that foundation (Bridgers 2016). The term "Jim Crow" originated in the 1820s, created by a white comedian named Thomas Rice. Rice created a character for minstrel shows that depicted what he found to be a stereotypical Black person. It was a derogatory representation, and the character's name (Jim Crow) became a nickname that was widely used for Black people (Andrews 2014).

During the era of Jim Crow laws, people who looked Black or were suspected of having Black ancestry were segregated. They weren't allowed to co-mingle with white people. At first, the laws required the separation of white people and Black people on public transportation and in schools (Blakemore 2020).

Eventually, segregation expanded beyond just transportation and schools. Co-mingling was also prohibited in cemeteries, parks, hospitals, churches, prisons, theaters, restaurants, and even bathrooms. Black people weren't even allowed to use the same drinking fountains as white people.

During the era of Jim Crow, facilities for Black people were underfunded, overcrowded, under-managed, and broken down compared to those offered to white people. Sometimes, the services and facilities offered to whites didn't even exist for Black people.

Hospitals were particularly under-resourced and overcrowded. Hospital staff were known to stop care mid-examination if they found out their patient had Black ancestry, forcing the patient to move to "colored" hospitals, even if the patient was likely to die from delayed care.

Can you imagine going to an emergency room and being told to leave because of how you looked? Even if leaving meant you'd die?

This was the reality for Black people across America.

During this time, Black people had the "legal right" to vote, but Jim Crow laws took away their practical ability to vote. States could impose taxes and literacy tests to prevent people from registering and voting, and they allowed all-white primaries (elections where only white people were allowed to vote) (Blakemore 2020).

Each state had different laws to uphold the racial hierarchy supported by local and state governments, some of them incredibly specific (Smithsonian National Museum of American History):

For instance, a 1930 law in Alabama prohibited white people from playing checkers with Black people.

A 1926 law in Georgia forbid Black barbers from cutting the hair of white women or girls.

A 1924 law in Maryland sentenced white women to a minimum of eighteen months in prison for carrying the child of a Black man (given what I've mentioned about lynchings earlier in this chapter, you can imagine what would happen to the Black man who fathered the child in such a scenario).

Even publicly supporting Black rights was a violation of some state laws. In Mississippi, a law was passed in 1920 prohibiting publicly supporting social equality for Black people or intermarriage between white and Black people.

White people who violated the Jim Crow laws were fined or imprisoned. Black people who violated the laws were often lynched—*without* the due process of law promised by the Fourteenth Amendment.

Our justice system was complicit in allowing these atrocities. Less than 1 percent of all lynchings after 1900 resulted in a lyncher receiving a criminal conviction of any kind (Equal Justice Initiative 2017).

The noose, a common weapon used during lynchings, is now recognized as a symbol of anti-Blackness, terror, and racial antagonism in America and *to this day* continues to be weaponized as a form of racial hatred and intolerance. In the spring of 2017, after Donald Trump won the 2016 presidential election, The National Museum of African American History and Culture at the Smithsonian released a statement that a noose had been hung outside of an exhibit that detailed the history of segregation in America. A few days later, a noose was found a short distance away from the museum (Held 2017).

I share all this to show that this country was built from the blood and bones of Black people, and for centuries, the government and society itself has consistently targeted this community with oppression, suppression, violence, and inequity.

The consistent brutalization of Black people as a collective group over the span of *centuries* was almost all-encompassing. And despite the discrimination, violence, and exclusionary immigration practices experienced by Asians prior to the civil rights movement, there is simply no equal comparison to the experience of Black people throughout American history.

And *that* was what Joshua was trying to get me to see all those years ago, during our conversation about my reaction to *The Vagina Monologues*. With all this history, we simply cannot compare the anti-Black racism Black people in America experience to the racism we as members of the South Asian diaspora in America have faced. This was what I failed to understand until I truly sat back and *listened*. Until I forced myself to examine my own prejudice and privilege and realized I was a mirror of the broader South Asian community.

CHAPTER 8

The Facts of Today I Didn't Know

Even with the Civil Rights Act of 1964 and the subsequent policies that ended the era of Jim Crow, discrimination and non-legalized systems of oppressing Black people are still an issue today.

Growing up, education was always pushed on me and the other youth in the community. Getting a "good" education is a central component of being a member of the "model minority." In fact, my research didn't reveal much anti-Asian discrimination in the education system in America.[3] Asian youth aren't systematically and systemically targeted by the education system in the same way Black youth are. We fly under the radar, assimilating and dedicating ourselves to our studies, getting a good education so the sacrifices our parents made coming to this country would be worth it.

---

3. This section focuses predominantly on the differences in experiences by white and Black children, since the research I found on racial disparities in the education system lacked data spotlighting discrimination against Asian children.

But there is a vast amount of research exploring the targeting of Black youth within the American education system.

Here are some quick facts on what the education system looks like for our Black counterparts (US Department of Education Office for Civil Rights 2014, 1):

- Black children represent only **18 percent** of preschool enrollment, but **48 percent** of preschool children receiving more than one out-of-school suspension are Black.
- Black students are suspended or expelled at a rate **three times greater** than white students.
- Black students only make up **16 percent** of the student enrollment but represent **31 percent** of students who are subjected to a school-related arrest.

What's crazy to me is that Black *preschoolers* are being disproportionately punished with suspension. This is critical because studies show high rates of suspension ultimately lead to higher rates of criminal activity and future imprisonment (National Institute of Justice 2021). From early childhood, Black youth are targeted disproportionately in a way that sets them up to struggle later in life.

This discrepancy in the way white students are treated compared to Black students speaks to the "thingification" Professor ross referred to in the previous chapter. In fact, research shows that while Black boys are punished for their actions, white boys *of the same age* are provided the assumption of innocence that is typically granted to children (Goff et al. 2014).

Black boys as young as *ten years old* are more likely to be mistaken as older than they are and are more likely to face police violence than white boys (Gilmore and Bettis 2021). What's more, researchers have found Black children are six times more likely than white children to be shot to death by the police (Badolato et al. 2020).

The Impact of Anti-Blackness on Black Children

The difference in the way society views Black children compared to its views of white children is referred to as "adultification."

Essentially, Black children are not given the same grace of childhood that white children are. Researchers have studied this phenomenon, finding Black children are often denied the grace of childhood and burdened with the culpability of adulthood. They are not given the leniency to grow and learn from childhood mistakes in the same way as their white peers. Black children are treated more harshly by school *and* criminal justice systems and experience excessive police force compared to white children (Gilmore and Bettis 2021).

Why is this important? Because Black parents around the country have to educate their *children* on how to handle interactions with authority—because authority figures may not actually see these kids as actual children and will treat them as adults. Having "The Talk" with your children is a necessary part of raising Black children in America (Solis 2021).

Mel told me once that his mother had a version of "The Talk" with him at a young age. "Don't believe everything they say about Black people in school," his mother had told him. "We come from kings and queens."

I learned "The Talk" often includes conversations Black parents have with their children on how to react to a police officer confronting them in the streets, on how to conduct themselves in a way to maximize their safety. It is a conversation centered around their racial identity and how to stay safe in a world that treats them differently than their white counterparts.

The unfortunate reality is we live in world where anti-Blackness isn't reserved only for Black adults. It is experienced by children who, by their very nature, should be symbols of innocence.

As allies to the Black community, it is critical for us to be aware of the "adultification" of Black children because it provides context for the stereotypes we see perpetuated about members of the Black community. This context is critical. If we see a high number of Black youth being arrested compared to their white counterparts, we have to ask ourselves *why*.

In the case of the school system, that "why" is because the school and legal systems have converged into what is called the school-to-prison pipeline (Bacher et al. 2019).

Professor Charles Bell, who teaches in the Department of Criminal Justice Sciences at Illinois State University and authored the book *Suspended: Punishment, Violence, and the Failure of School Safety*, offered me his time during the process of researching for this book.

Professor Bell explained that zero-tolerance policies (which require strict punishment for certain behaviors, regardless of context) in certain schools and the high presence of law enforcement at these schools has created a pattern of tracking students out of school and into criminal justice systems.

Zero-tolerance policies essentially allow schools to rely on the juvenile justice system for student behaviors that were once handled by the schools themselves. Essentially, instead of being sent to a school counselor for acting out in school, kids get tracked into juvenile court (Camera 2021).

And who do you think gets targeted the most by officers at these school? Black students. Where do you think the schools with armed officers tend to be? In predominantly Black neighborhoods.

What's more, not only are Black students more likely to be criminalized in school but they are also more likely to attend schools with fewer resources and school staff than their white counterparts. Staff at these schools are often not adequately trained and are usually already overworked and underpaid. These schools typically lack support staff qualified to address behavioral problems.

Prior to writing this book, even I was unaware of just how unequal the education system in America is.

What blew my mind was how closely discrimination in *housing* impacted the quality of resources in *schools*. The interlocking of discriminatory practices across the board are truly mind-boggling.

Growing up, I took so many things in school for granted. Access to guidance counselors, computers, books, supplies, even well maintained buildings: for students in my neighborhood, these resources were all funded by local property taxes.

Property taxes for different areas are impacted by the value of the homes in those areas. We had access to all these resources because the schools we went to were in predominantly white areas. As a result, these areas had higher property values. Higher property values mean higher property taxes. This taxpayer money is then allocated to school resources.

In lower-income areas, home values are lower, so fewer taxes are collected—which means less money for school resources.

Schools in low-income neighborhoods receive less funding and oftentimes can't afford updated textbooks, building repairs, or basic school supplies (let alone the digital whiteboards I saw in my high school or the high-tech computer labs we were privileged to use). They have larger class sizes, higher suspension and expulsion rates, and higher faculty turnover.

Black youth continue to face inequalities in the education system even after graduating high school. Black students who graduate from college have more debt than their white counterparts, and they are twice as likely to be unemployed compared to white students (Scott and Li 2016). Research has shown Black graduates face job discrimination after college. In fact, job applicants who had "white" names were 50 percent more likely to be contacted for job interviews than applicants who had "Black" names (Bertrand 2016).

Anti-Blackness Impacts Home Ownership in the Black Community

During my research, I learned there is a connection between racism, schools, property values, and home ownership; all these things are intertwined.

There are reasons that property values in Black neighborhoods are lower than in white neighborhoods. There are reasons why schools in predominantly Black areas don't have the funding they need for adequate school resources. One of these reasons is called redlining.

During the Great Depression, the Federal Housing Administration used maps to figure out what areas would be guaranteed mortgages. The Home Owners' Loan Corporation assessed risk predominantly based on the racial composition of the neighborhood. Non-white neighborhoods were considered "hazardous" and colored red, hence the term "redlining." People who lived in these "hazardous" areas were deemed financially risky, and homes in areas deemed "hazardous" also suffered from lower property values.

Redlining denied people of color, particularly Black people, access to mortgage refinancing and federal loans. Black families were unable to acquire the financing options necessary to purchase their own homes and were also financially prevented from moving to areas with higher property values (Gross 2017).

This is relevant because about 74 percent of the neighborhoods redlined in the 1930s are to this day low-to-moderate income neighborhoods. More than 60 percent are still predominantly communities of color (Mitchell 2018).

What all this means is the government has directly undermined the ability of Black communities to build wealth by historically limiting the community's ability to engage in home ownership.

Discrimination in the housing market is still prevalent today. For example, in 2017, 45 percent of Black people (compared to 25 percent of Asian Americans) experienced discrimination when trying to buy or rent a house (Social Science Research Solutions 2017). Mortgage lenders continue to target people of color with risky and speculative loans that have high interest rates.

Racial bias also continues to impact property values. A federally commissioned report released in 2022 found homes in Black communities are significantly undervalued compared to similar homes in non-Black neighborhoods. In fact, homes in predominantly Black neighborhoods are undervalued by almost $50,000 (National Fair Housing Alliance 2022).

Redlining and racial bias in the housing market have contributed to neighborhoods that are segregated by race. These neighborhoods are not just the result of groups of people from similar backgrounds choosing to live together. They are also the result of housing policies that have made it so people in these areas simply can't afford to live anywhere else. Further, housing segregation leads to issues of accessibility because businesses determine where to operate based on demographics. If businesses do not think certain areas have the economic means to support them, they will choose to open operations in more affluent areas.

Access to parks, restaurants, grocery stores, well maintained roads, and any number of things we take for granted: these are all impacted by racial bias. When I lived in New York City and worked in East Harlem, I would notice the stark contrast in restaurants and businesses operating in Harlem compared to the options near my apartment on the Upper East Side. I had a Fairway grocery store and Whole Foods Market as well as dozens and dozens of eateries within walking distance of my apartment. By work, my options were limited to bodegas and fast food.

A conversation on home ownership is critical to the topic of anti-Blackness because home ownership runs parallel to wealth accumulation. In 2021, only 44 percent of Black households owned their homes. Seventy-four percent of white households own their homes, and almost 60 percent of Asian households own their homes (Duffin 2022).

Other Inequities[4]

There's so many more ways Black people in this country have suffered because of systemic racism that entire graduate-level courses are dedicated to discussing them. I can only touch upon a handful of them in this book, but I encourage you to explore the resources provided at the end of this book to learn more.

Here are some fast facts:

Black women are almost four times more likely than white and Asian women to die from pregnancy-related causes (Centers for Disease Control and Prevention 2022).

Black babies have an infant mortality rate that is 2.3 times greater than that of white babies, and they are four times more likely to die from complications than white babies. Infant mortality of Asian babies was the lowest of any other racial group (Ellie and Driscoll 2020, 3).

Black households are 2.5 times more likely to experience food insecurity than white households. In 2021, one out of five Black households experienced food insecurity (which is defined as lack of certainty regarding the ability to feed members of the household) (Coleman-Jensen et al. 2022, 19).

Black men are almost five times more likely to be imprisoned than white men. Government studies have also found that Black people will serve longer sentences *for the same crimes* committed by white people. They also have a higher chance of being killed during an encounter with law

---

4. There is little research specifically comparing the different experiences of Black and Asian people in America, so many of these statistics compare Black experiences to their white counterparts. For instance, there is limited data on food insecurity in the Asian population compared to the Black population.

enforcement. Studies show bias against Black men in the criminal justice system, and policies like mandatory minimums lead to harsher prison sentences for the Black community specifically (Nellis 2021). The school-to-prison pipeline and the adultification of Black youth also contribute to the high rates of Black men in prisons.

Finally, Black people have been policed so thoroughly in America that even their *hair* has been seen as threatening (Butler 2020). A 2021 study found Black women who wore their hair in braids, cornrows, afros, or other hairstyles were perceived as being less professional compared to Black women who straightened their hair (Koyal and Rosette 2021).

In March 2022, the CROWN Act (Creating a Respectful and Open World for Natural Hair) was passed in California to protect Black people from hair discrimination. The bill states, "Routinely, people of African descent are deprived of educational and employment opportunities because they are adorned with natural or protective hairstyles in which hair is tightly coiled or tightly curled, or worn in locs, cornrows, twists, braids, Bantu knots or Afros." The bill is meant to prevent employers from firing or discriminating against workers based on their hair texture or style.

I hope you can see how problematic it is that the intensity of discrimination against Black people in this country is so deep that a law was literally passed to protect Black people so they can wear their hair the way it naturally grows out of their heads and not worry about acquiring or losing their jobs.

How 2020 Shone a Light on My Own Blind Spots

I hope this chapter gave a little bit of insight into just how *different* it is to have generational trauma as a Black person in this country and how anti-Blackness and the racism we experience as South Asians in America simply cannot be compared.

This difference in the respective experiences of the Asian and Black communities in this country was truly brought to the forefront of my awareness in 2020.

In February 2020, I was sitting in the waiting room of my doctor's office, waiting to get my blood drawn for a wellness exam. I was scrolling through my news feed and a headline caught my eye. A young Black man had been jogging down a residential street and was shot dead by white men. Ahmaud Arbery was twenty-five when he was killed, chased by white men in their trucks and murdered because of the color of his skin. I remember my eyes burning and my nose dripping as I cried in the waiting room, thinking about the fear he must have felt in the moments before his death.

I went home that morning and curled into Mel's arms, kissing the skin along his shoulders, kissing his face and his hands. I squeezed him tightly, and he held me, comforting me. "Are you scared?" I'd asked him.

"No," he said, holding me against him. "Why would I be scared?"

"Because a Black man was killed by white men for doing nothing but going for a jog. It's 2020. This shouldn't still be happening." I felt Mel's chest rumble as he spoke, his voice deep and thoughtful as he spoke into my hair.

"Babe, I've been Black my entire life. This isn't new to me. This doesn't shock me or surprise me. It pisses me off. But

I learned a long time ago that I can't live in fear. I wouldn't be able to function."

He began to share stories with me from his youth. One story he shared made my stomach twist and my heart ache. He told me how, when he was living in San Diego, police officers removed him from his car and handcuffed him, shoving him against a car for "looking suspicious" and "loitering" in front of a convenience store. He was released when the manager of the convenience store arrived and intervened. Mel had arrived early to his shift at the convenience store. He was in college and hoping to make manager, so he always showed up early to his shifts.

He also told me about the time a white man in a pickup truck drove by him as he waited at a bus stop on his way to class at the local college. Barack Obama was running for president, and Mel's neighborhood was politically divided. The man slowed down as he drove by, made a gun with his two fingers, and pretended to shoot Mel. Mel stared him down, and the man smirked and drove away.

He'd never shared these kinds of stories with me before, and I cried as he spoke. I was so *ignorant*. I loved this man so deeply, and there was so much about his life experiences I still didn't know.

We began discussing his experiences as I asked more and more questions, every story culminating in a new series of questions. And they only increased as time went by, as more news stories broke highlighting violence against Black people.

In March 2020, Breonna Taylor was killed in her home by police officers. In May 2020, George Floyd was killed by Derek Chauvin as a Hmong American officer, Tou Thao, stood by.

Tou Thao's complicity in George Floyd's murder reverberated throughout the Asian American community. As I observed the tidal wave of reaction through the media, I began to see how I had been complicit in the anti-Blackness activists were highlighting in the Asian American community. For many people who identify as Asian American, George Floyd's death was a catalyst to unpacking the prejudice and anti-Blackness in our own communities.

As activists and politicians across the country spoke out against George Floyd's death and shone a spotlight on police brutality, I listened more closely than I likely would have had I not been in a relationship with a Black man.

I typed that last sentence intentionally because part of self-growth is self-acceptance and self-awareness. The reality is George Floyd's death would have upset me, it would have grated at me, and it would have angered me regardless of Mel's presence in my life.

And yes, I would have listened to the voices that spoke out against anti-Blackness, I would have reflected on my own contribution to the problem, and I would have sought to educate myself so I could be a better ally (or, to be honest, so I could actually *become* an ally to begin with). But I cannot truthfully say the severity of the impact George Floyd's death had on my life would have been the same had I not been in a relationship with a Black man, had I not planned on starting a family with this man.

I cannot say awareness of police brutality against Black men would have haunted me as deeply, that it would have stolen so many nights of sleep, if I was not scared for my partner's life when he walked out of our home every day. As the Black Lives Matter movement gained traction and Black Lives Matter protesters were met with violence, I worried tirelessly over the safety of my partner. And, for the first time in my life, I became aware of the fear Black parents feel for the safety of their children.

In the summer of 2020, my heart broke for every Black parent in America, past, present, and future. Because my fear over my partner must have paled in comparison to the fear generations of Black parents have felt for their children, particularly during periods of political divide.

It was that summer I began peeling back yet another layer of myself to challenge what aspects of my childhood prejudice I still retained. I thought I had gone through such an evolution after all the time I spent with Sabina. I had no idea just how much work I still had to do on myself. It was not easy, constantly self-analyzing and pushing myself out of my comfort zone.

2020 was a very challenging year. The growing pains were uncomfortable as hell. But it was only then that I truly realized how much I still had to learn about the Black experience in America.

Part 4

CHAPTER 9

The Problematic "Me"

It was not until my midtwenties, when I made the decision to walk away from my community and my marriage, that I was able to put a name to the preference for "whiteness" I'd witnessed my entire life. That preference is known as "colorism," and it is woven into anti-Black racism in America.

Colorism, at its most basic level, is a value system of favoring lighter-colored skin over darker-colored skin. Though it is often observed in people from the same race or ethnic group, colorism can be observed across racial groups. It follows the mentality of "light is right."

My decision to leave my marriage and to essentially ostracize myself from my family was a self-induced shock to my system. I knew there were things I did not know, and the only way to grow into a more self-actualized and better version of myself was to rip myself away from the protection of my comfortably ignorant world.

As I became more educated and exposed myself to people from different races and cultures, I learned that the compliments Ravi would bestow upon me were inherently colorist.

I remember sitting next to him on a beach in Santa Monica, the moon bright against a deeply dark night sky, listening to the waves hit the shore. We'd walked a distance from the pier to get away from the light pollution. We'd been together for almost six months, and I was still giddy with new love.

"Tell me again why you wanted to talk to me when you first saw me," I asked him, leaning into his warm body. I looked up at him, admiring the long lashes that framed his big eyes. I could drown in those deep brown eyes, and I spent many an evening staring into them, mesmerized by this man who had stolen my heart.

He chuckled as he wrapped his arm tighter around me, pulling me closer into his side.

"I was sitting in the back of the lecture hall, and I saw this girl walk in wearing a bright green jacket and brown shorts. Her skin was light, and I could tell she had big eyes even from how far away I was. And when she turned, I liked the shape of her nose." He flicked a finger across the tip of my nose. "She looked Persian. She looked like she might be part *gori*. And so I sought her out, and now she's my girlfriend."

He kissed my cheek, and we nuzzled into each other. As I look back at this sweet, beautiful moment through the eyes of adulthood, through the eyes of a woman who has seen more of the world and experienced more of its people, I cringe. I loved Ravi deeply. He was, at one point in my life, my best friend. It was oftentimes painful to write about him for this book, knowing that the image the reader would absorb of him would not be favorable.

And a part of me aches that much our relationship is now shadowed by my knowledge of just how deeply problematic so many of the values we shared as a couple truly are. Ravi was, when I knew him, a good man who was simply the by-product of his upbringing. And part of that upbringing included a preference for lighter skin, for the elevation of "whiteness." It is why he would compliment me by calling me "*gori*."

The term "*gori*" refers to a white woman. When he told me I looked like I might be *gori*, he essentially told me I looked like I might be multiracial.

More bluntly, my skin color, its lightness, was what initially caught Ravi's attention. It was what first sparked his interest. There were other compliments that, in hindsight, were problematic.

I recall our evening walks, where he'd put his finger to my cheek when we'd stand under a streetlamp, waiting for the crosswalk light to change, and lovingly say, "*Gori laghdeeya*." Translated into English, these words mean, "You look fair-skinned," or, for a more literal translation, "You look like a white woman."

We lay in the grass one cool summer evening in spring, and he played me one of his favorite songs. *Gori Teri Aankhen* by an artist named Lucky Ali. The singer serenades his love, crooning lyrics that translate into "White girl, your eyes are telling me that last night you didn't sleep at all." "White girl" could be interchanged with "fair-skinned girl," but the result is the same. The singer is smitten with a light-skinned woman, and the word "*gori*" is a term of endearment.

Funnily enough, my lighter skin was the result of me spending most of my time indoors. Despite living in Southern California, my skin remained the pale hue of a college student who spent most of her free time in libraries or in her dorm room studying. As the years went by, and I spent more time with my nose out of my schoolbooks, my skin became a richer brown, touched by the sun and heat. It was an unavoidable reality. But "luckily," according to my ex, my tan was more gold, so it was "still" pretty (the implicit suggestion being that it would not be his preference for my tan to *not* have that golden hue). My mother has lighter skin, as her ancestry includes European lineage, and Ravi was grateful for that. He'd often comment on the fairness of my mother's skin.

But even my "gold" skin needed to become fair again before I got married. Six months before my wedding, I purchased a wide-brimmed hat that I wore everywhere, so I would stay pale and fair for our wedding. Neither of us wanted me to look too brown in my photographs. The most beautiful brides were those who were "fair and lovely," which was actually the name of one of the most popular skin-lightening lotions sold in India. "Fair & Lovely" (which now goes by "Glow & Lovely") was Unilever's best-selling product in India.

Though I grew up criticizing the "Fair & Lovely" advertisements I'd see on the Indian channels my grandparents watched, I criticized them not because of their attempts to hock "fairness" to consumers but because their representations of the "before" and "after" photos were so unrealistic. There's no way a woman could get *that* many shades lighter just from using a lotion! Also, they weren't "naturally" light-skinned. Therefore, their beauty wasn't "natural" and was inferior to a woman who was born naturally fair-skinned.

This mentality was the result of an ever-present need to judge other people. Whether it is financial success, educational background, or a person's outward presentation, my culture is one that criticizes harshly. I grew up receiving harsh judgment, and I in turn learned how to give it, a part of a generational cycle of unwarranted criticism.

In fact, I ended a friendship with a Gujarati friend in college because I was constantly judged and criticized for the smallest things. It would only be years later that I realized I did the exact same thing to my own loved ones that she did to me.

And it is only with hindsight that I see my complicity in colorism went far back into my childhood. Growing up, my younger cousin's skin would darken in the sun, an almost umber skin tone that would last all summer and get deeper and richer every time she spent time in the pool. The adults (even my uncle and aunt, her own parents) would taunt her, teasing her about her darkness.

"*Kahli*," they'd taunt. "You got so dark!"

I remember being in middle school, watching as my cousin fell to the floor crying as the teasing heightened after one particularly long bout in the pool. I remember feeling guilty for laughing, vaguely knowing even then that something wasn't quite right about the situation. But the adults were the ones mocking her, so it must have been okay.

I knew how awful it felt to get teased by my family. I was mercilessly teased for any number of things, including getting darker in the sun. It was all normal to me. So if I had to deal with it, it made sense to me that other girls in my family did too.

My family wasn't the only family who made pointed criticisms about their children's skin tones. I routinely heard comments about Ravi's sister.

Ravi's younger sister is a beautiful woman. Though I haven't seen her in many years, I am confident her beauty has only blossomed as she's aged. Thick, luscious curly hair spilled down her back, and she had large almond-shaped eyes with long lashes. She was, as I think back on her, one of the most beautiful girls I've ever seen.

But even she was ruthlessly critiqued, as her skin was many shades darker than my own.

"Ankita could be a model if she wasn't so dark," Ravi once told me. Every summer when I'd visit his family home, I'd hear his mother (who is, to this day, one of the sweetest, kindest souls I've ever known) and Ravi comment on her darkened summer skin.

And I, of course, would comfort myself that even though I wasn't as beautiful as my sister-in-law, at least I wasn't as dark as she was. It sickens me to even type that out, but I had thoroughly subscribed to the colorist value system I'd witnessed in my community growing up. The values of my community and family had imprinted themselves deeply on my impressionable mind.

The anecdotes I can share are endless.

One that makes me cringe and recoil from the past version of myself involves a conversation with Ravi and his sister. We were discussing how cute we thought mixed-race babies were.

The cuteness of a mixed-race child was heightened if the baby was "half-white." "Half-white" babies were the "cutest." Even "half-white, half-Indian" babies were cuter than "full-blooded" Indian babies. Because the whiteness softened the brown, diluted the melanin. It was as if we wanted to hold onto the richness and depth of our culture while also wanting to dilute the gold in our own blood, to wash out the flavor in our own skin.

"I hope our baby is fair," Ravi would say. And I'd wholeheartedly agree with him.

I reflected upon these memories as I was pregnant, while my baby, who received half of its DNA from Mel, grew in my belly. As I wrote of my memories about the mixed-race babies, my eyes were wet with frustration and disgust.

The unfortunate truth is that these stories are but a microcosm of my culture as a whole.

CHAPTER 10

Colorism in South Asian Culture

India (and arguably the majority of Asian countries more broadly) is a rampantly colorist country, and colorism is also a thick thread woven throughout the Indian diaspora. As I type this, I can already hear the voices clamoring to protest my words. One of the aspects of the Indian community (or really any community) I find particularly amusing is a perspective that if a good number of people *don't* believe in something, their lack of belief cancels out the reality of the larger masses that *do* believe in that same thing.

"Not all Indians favor light skin" or "Not all South Asians are racist, please stop generalizing" are comments I've seen on social media platforms and in the comments sections of online articles I've read and personally written.

No, not all South Asians are racist or colorist, but enough are that it's a very real problem. Enough are that artists produce hit songs like "Chittiyan Kalaiyan" (an absurd song about a man who goes into a tizzy seeing the "white" wrists of his love interest) and "Chura Ke Dil Mera Goriya Chali" (wherein the male singer is "driven crazy" by the whiteness of his love's skin). Both these songs were considered hits in 2021. Hell, there's even a popular song simply called "Gori Gori"—which literally means "white girl white girl."

And, no, not all South Asians are racist or colorist, but enough are that Unilever can continue to sell "Glow & Lovely" without changing its formula, without hurting its sales, because people know the "pink glow" the newly branded product offers in its revamped messaging is just another way to market skin lightening. In fact, the international market for skin whitening cosmetics is predicted to reach more than $6.5 billion by 2025 (Global Industry Analysts).

Up until 2020, the globally popular "Glow & Lovely" lotion notoriously only featured light-skinned brown women (or darker-skinned brown women who had their skin lightened with editing) and used to also include shade cards so consumers could determine how "fair" their skin tone could become from using the lotion. While Unilever continues to sell "Glow & Lovely," Johnson & Johnson pulled its skin-lightening products from the market after the murder of George Floyd sparked an international conversation about racial inequality and brought light to the reality of colorism on a global scale (McEvoy 2020).

Interestingly, Johnson & Johnson's product lines "Fine Fairness" by Neutrogena and "Clear Fairness" by Clean & Clear were only distributed in Asia and the Middle East, which both have cultures deeply committed to colorism (Schild 2020).

Furthermore, colorism in Indian culture specifically is so pervasive that it appears in something as innocuous as naming a crayon color. For example, a large company called Hindustan Pencils in India manufactures a popular brand of pencils and crayons. One of their products, the Colorado crayon series, has a peach-colored crayon labeled "skin." In a country whose populace has a widely varied skin color spectrum that tends toward being darker skinned, this company has taken a light, peach-colored crayon and called it "skin." The product itself will predominantly be used by children, children who at a very tender age can internalize the message that "skin" is a light peach color.

In 2013, a twenty-two-year-old college student in India tried to sue the company to get the name of the crayon changed, and the student lost (Vyas 2014). A smaller company (Navneet) did change the name of their peach-colored crayon from "flesh" to "peach" (Johari 2015). Interestingly, Crayola's peach-colored crayon was once also named "flesh," but the company changed it to "peach" in 1962 in response to the civil rights movement in the United States. Crayola now has a set of crayons representing different skin tones.

Moreover, India's film industry is a glaring culprit in perpetuating colorism within Indian culture and community. As recently as 2020, a film called *Khaali Peeli* received backlash for containing a song with lyrics that roughly translated to, "Just by watching you, oh fair-skinned girl, Beyoncé will be ashamed." It's not fully clear if the song is suggesting Beyoncé will be ashamed because the dancing girl is *just as good* of a dancer as her, except lighter in skin tone, or if the fair-skinned dancing girl is a *better* dancer than Beyoncé.

After the song was called out for its racist undertones, the director of the film (and writer of the song), Maqbool Khan, released a statement stating that the term *"goriya"* was not meant to be used literally but was meant to be used as a synonym to the word "girl." He stated, "There is no derogation intended. I assure you that the lyric in question was never intended racially. In fact, the term 'goriya' has been so often and traditionally used in Indian songs to address a girl, that it didn't occur to any of us to interpret it in the literal manner" (Srivastava 2020).

Though his statement was meant to mollify listeners who were offended by the racist undertones of the song, it is incredibly problematic. It brings to light just how deeply rooted colorism is in Indian culture. The word used for a "fair" girl has become a *synonym* for the word "girl" more generally speaking. It has become a term of endearment, of affection. No such word is used popularly to describe a dark-skinned woman, a medium-toned woman—only the fair-skinned woman.

Indian's film industry, Bollywood, is the largest producer of film in the world. Its influence on societal ideas of beauty, therefore, is unquestionable. Bollywood is notorious for favoring light-skinned actors and actresses, so much so that filmmakers will utilize "brownface" in their films to depict characters of darker skin color, instead of hiring darker-skinned people.

In 2019, the film *Bala* came under scrutiny for making the horribly ironic decision to hire a well-known actress named Bhumi Pednekar to play a character who suffers discrimination based on her skin tone. The irony is that Pednekar darkened her skin to play the role. Instead of hiring a darker-skinned actress to play the role of a character who experiences prejudice and discrimination because of the darkness of her skin, Bollywood hired a lighter-skinned actress and artificially darkened her skin.

Two other films, *Super 30* and *Gully Boy*, also joined Bala in 2019 as films that used brownface. In *Super 30*, actor Hrithik Roshan plays a teacher from Bihar, one of India's more economically challenged states. Though the filmmakers decided a character from a poorer state should have dark skin, they didn't think a darker-skinned person deserved the opportunity to actually play the role. Instead, it was given to a lighter-skinned megastar who would help the film make more sales.

And consumers of Bollywood films endorse the use of brownface by paying to see these movies. While accurate box office figures are difficult to obtain in India, *Gully Boy*, *Bala*, and *Super 30* were reportedly among the twenty-five highest-grossing Bollywood movies in 2019. All three used brownface (Box Office India).

Essentially, South Asian culture's attachment to fairness is as alive today as it's ever been.

In 2020, Netflix released a series called *Indian Matchmaking*. Throughout the show, Sima Aunty, the show's matchmaker, constantly comments on how the most successful marriage matches happen for women who are "tall, fair, and trim." Even an American-born Indian woman on the show asks for a match that is "not too dark, you know… fair-skinned."

Indian Matchmaking was a hit when it was released on Netflix. While it brought into public spotlight the reality of colorism in our culture, the producers of the show did little to engage viewers in dialogue about the colorism evident in the show. In Season Two, discussions of skin tone were notably absent.

Given this adherence to skin tone preference, it's no surprise to see colorism evident on the website for an online Indian matchmaking service. The website, Shaadi.com, is now a global app popular not only in its core market (India, Pakistan, and Bangladesh) but also on an international level. I personally know individuals who have used it who live in

Canada, the United Kingdom, and the United States. The app allowed subscribers to filter potential matches by skin tone. They could screen out matches based on whether they were "fair," "wheatish," or "dark."

When I first learned this, I was appalled but not surprised. After my divorce, when I was single and dating in New York City, I was in a bar talking to a very handsome brown man. He was funny and charming, and he told me how beautiful I was a number of times. My beauty, however, couldn't compete with the incredibly fair-skinned Indian woman who walked into the bar behind me.

"I work in a clinic uptown," I said, feeling my words trail off as I noticed his attention had shifted to someone behind me. I turned my head and saw a tall, slim woman walk in with a group of brown women who all seemed to be Indian. Her skin was fairer than my mother's own incredibly fair skin. Even her eyes seemed shades lighter than my own.

"Now *that's* a queen," the man in front of me said softly under his breath. "Excuse me."

And then he was gone, walking away from me toward the lighter-skinned woman.

It was one of the first and only times in my life I have ever looked at another Indian woman and felt unworthy in comparison, exclusively based on our skin colors. In a single moment, I realized how absurd and petty my feelings over my ex-sister-in-law had been, and how truly ridiculous it was for me to find any sense of security in myself based on my skin color.

As the anti-racism protests of the summer of 2020 garnered global attention, a number of individuals petitioned to have Shaadi.com remove its skin tone filter in solidarity with the anti-racism movement (Mahtani 2020). The skin filter is no longer available on the website or app, but the reality is as recently as 2020 we could pick and choose which people on the internet we wanted to date purely on the basis of their skin tone.

CHAPTER 11

The Impact of Casteism and Colonialism on Anti-Blackness

A thorough explanation for the Indian caste system is beyond the scope of this book and beyond my ability to provide, given the incredible intricacies involved in the evolution of caste as we know it today. Despite not having an expertise on this topic, I wrote this chapter to offer a high-level background on how casteism, colonialism, and anti-Blackness may emerge in the lives of members of the South Asian diaspora. As I researched for this chapter, I had the privilege of speaking to prabhdeep singh kehal, a sociologist of racism and colonialism. Dr. kehal studies how racism and colonialism are practiced among elite individuals and organizations in the U.S., and they offered their knowledge on the history of caste evolution throughout the Asian subcontinent. Dr. kehal also helped inform my understanding of the relationship between caste, colorism, and anti-Blackness as I began the process of writing this book.

The caste system observed throughout the Asian subcontinent today is incredibly complicated. It differs by faith, region, and country because different histories inform how casteism shows up in each culture within South Asia. There are a multitude of theories about the historic establishment of the caste system, but they all have to do with how power is maintained in specific societies over time.

The "true" origins of the South Asian caste system are regularly debated. Scholars offer religious, biological, and social theories to explain the origins, but they have come to no uniform consensus (in fact, different forms of casteism are even present within the present-day African continent). Some historians suggest the global origins of caste may be traced to what is present-day India.

At a high level, the reigning caste system in India divides people (specifically Hindus) into four main groups: Brahmins, Kshatriyas, Vaishyas, and Shudras. The Brahmins are at the top of the hierarchy and are known to be the intellectuals, the legislators, or the priests. They are hierarchically followed by the Kshatriyas, who are the rulers or warriors of society. The Vaishyas come third, and they are the traders and merchants of society. At the bottom of the hierarchy are the Shudras, and they are typically viewed as peasants who are responsible for filling "menial" jobs (Equality Labs 2018).

These four main castes are then subdivided into thousands of other castes, but outside of all this exists a group of humans who are not even considered part of the caste system itself: the Dalits (as they self-identify in the present). Formerly referred to as "untouchables," those who are considered Dalits do not even warrant a spot within the hierarchy and are still considered "untouchable" within contemporary societies. In certain parts of South Asia, Dalits continue to be segregated from society, forced to attend segregated schools and places of worship, and experience violent aggression (Biswas 2020).

India's constitution banned caste-based discrimination (and the government even implemented quotas in government jobs and educational institutions to correct the injustices of the caste system), but caste preference is still practiced. In its 2019 "World Report," Human Rights Watch revealed that Dalits continued to suffer from discrimination in education and the workforce. Violence against Dalits globally has also increased, possibly because of activism advocating against the caste systems that oppress and dehumanize them (Human Rights Watch 2019).

Adherence to caste ideologies also plays a role in sexual violence against women. For example, Dalit women are some of the most oppressed people *in the world*, and they experience high rates of sexual violence (Biswas 2020). Essentially, the caste system allows those who follow it to dehumanize Dalit women so much so that sexual violence against them often goes unchecked. Dalit women are, on a global level, "thingified," just as the Black community was "thingified" for so much of American history.

Furthermore, discrimination against Dalits is so pervasive that anti-Dalit sentiment is strong enough to cross oceans. In 2020, Cisco was sued by California's Department of Fair Employment and Housing on the basis of caste discrimination. The codefendents of the lawsuit were Indian supervisors who allegedly hazed and bullied a Dalit engineer because of his caste status (Iyengar 2020).

Caste Preference Persists

While it may seem like an ideological relic of the past, caste is still an active consideration for many South Asians today.

I had a brief friendship in college with a girl whose family immigrated from Sri Lanka, and I remember giggling with her over her forbidden love (dating was looked down upon in her family, as most of the marriages in her family were typically arranged). One of her concerns with her newly discovered love was that he was of a lower caste than her family. Despite her entire family now living as part of the South Asian diaspora in the United States, caste was still a concern for them as she considered a life partner.

Years later, I sat in an Italian restaurant with my friend Malika, who grew up in Bombay. We were finishing up our first year of graduate school at Columbia, and she wanted to celebrate with a nice meal and glass of wine. Malika came from a wealthy family in India and her accent was more British than Indian, as she'd gone to esteemed British schools her entire life. We began discussing the issue of poverty in the States, as the class we had just left centered around community nutrition.

"What's it like in India? The level of poverty there?" I'd asked her, as I hadn't yet visited India. My father and grandparents went often but hesitated to bring me for reasons I still don't truly understand.

"Dude," she said, dipping her bread into the garlicky olive oil poured into the plate in front of me. "It's so bad, but, to be honest, I don't even notice it anymore."

"Really?" I asked, sipping my wine and looking at her face as she rolled her eyes.

"Dude, you don't get it. They're everywhere. We call them the untouchables. The kids will come and ask you for money all the time, and I just ignore them. If you give one of them food or money, the rest flock around you as if they are starving pigeons. So you have to ignore them. They don't really exist to me. So it's interesting to me that Americans are so concerned with the homeless population. Like, we don't really care in India. It's just part of life."

I shook my head. "But don't you feel bad? Seeing all those poor people when you have so much?"

"No. My dad works really hard for what we have. We can't save everyone. It is just the way things are. I don't think about it too much. Let's talk about something else. We're supposed to be celebrating!"

Though I honored her request to talk about something else, it was odd that Malika wanted to change topics so quickly. We had just spent four months in a class that focused on the impacts of poverty on food access and behaviors within the United States and had spent hours together having discussions on the things we'd learned from the course. When I tried to talk about poverty in India, however, she shut down within a couple of minutes of conversation.

Though she readily acknowledged her awareness of and participation in the caste system (she said "we call them untouchables" and "they don't really exist to me," which made me realize *she* also saw them as "untouchables"), she didn't actually want to engage in conversation about it.

A year after we had that conversation, Malika moved back home to India, and her family hired a matchmaker to find a suitable husband for her—finding a man from her same caste was a nonnegotiable for her family.

Just as Malika showed disinterest or aversion to discussing her participation in casteism, so too did my family sidestep my questions when I tried to dig in deeper to what the caste system meant to our community.

Even as a child, I knew my family was proud to be *jatt*. *Jatts* are a group of people who are part of a landowning feudal system in Punjab. Though this system is technically intertwined with the Hindu caste system, it operates differently because of how it evolved in Punjab (the caste system operates differently throughout Asia but also throughout present-day India). Though my family is Sikh and was therefore supposed to denounce ties to casteism, we were all very attached to our *jatt* heritage. I grew up listening to bhangra music about *jatt* pride, and when my family learned Ravi was also *jatt* our union became that much more desirable. My family's *jatt* pride mirrored that of many Punjabi Sikhs in our community. My grandfather would tell me that we were landowners, that in Punjab we were considered the highest caste because owning land meant we had power.

Because our surnames identified us as *jatts*, members of my immediate community kept their surnames. Many orthodox Sikhs discard their surnames in order to separate themselves from caste hierarchies (as it is a tenet in Sikh faith to denounce caste), but as a child I was told Punjabi Sikhs who have discarded their surnames are not *jatts* (because why would you not want the world to know you are a member of the landowning caste?).

Because of the *jatt* pride in my community (and the fact that the pride seemed to come from a feeling of superiority versus a love of actual land), I was indoctrinated into a hierarchical approach to viewing other people at a very young age.

How Does Caste Play a Role in Anti-Blackness?

Scholars suggest that the history of colorism in India (and other South Asian countries) may have been profoundly influenced by the variances in skin tones resulting from the division of societal roles. Over generations, those who toiled outside would naturally get darker skin from working outside under the sun, compared to those who owned land and remained indoors. Skin tone thus became an important marker for distinguishing to which caste people belonged. Families with darker skin were assumed to be laborers (and therefore of lower caste status) who worked the soil that belonged to the fairer-skinned landowners, who stayed inside and ensured their property would be inherited across generations. These fairer-skinned landowners held a higher caste status.

Thus, over time, darker skin became associated with lower caste status than fair skin.

European colonialism also had an impact on color preference via the colonizers' preferential treatment of certain castes. For instance, when British colonial leaders arrived in India in the nineteenth century, whatever color prejudice existed as a result of casteism deepened because the British were able to use caste divisions as part of their colonial rule to manage different communities and keep them apart. Over time, a hierarchy was further institutionalized between the fair skin of the colonizers and the darker skin of the colonized.

When the British Raj established rule in India in 1858, the British implemented an institutionalized form of segregation (Kaul 2011). Some institutions discriminated against all Indians, while others only discriminated against "black

Indians" (with signs that read "No dogs or Indians" outside of restaurants and other establishments) (Bhangle 2020).

Lighter-skinned Indians were given more job opportunities and were treated preferentially compared to their darker-skinned counterparts. I grew up reading stories by Rudyard Kipling (the British author who wrote *The Jungle Book*), but it was only as an adult that I became aware of his reflections on British imperialism, wherein he highlights the differences between the white colonizers and the "uncivilized" Indians they conquered.

Indian culture's predilection for fair skin wasn't something I ever truly questioned as a child, and its emphasis on caste hierarchy wasn't something I found peculiar or unwarranted. It was as "normal" a part of my culture as afternoon *chaa*, with everyone around me engaging and seemingly attached to the ritual. I accepted this predilection and adopted it myself for years, ignorant to the hypocrisy, fallacy, and irony of calling myself a Sikh *jatt*.

The impact of the caste system and the repercussions of India's colonial history weren't made clear to me until I began to question my culture's predilection for "whiteness," until I left my marriage and essentially walked away from my Indian community in a desperate attempt to "find myself."

Understanding the possible roots of colorism has not only helped me challenge my own anxieties about my skin tone—one of my best friends calls me a sun baby now, as I lie out in the sun, embracing the warmth and enjoying my skin becoming deeper and more bronze each summer—but has also shed light on why members of my community may hold implicit and/or unconscious bias against the Black community in America.

If my culture is so deeply committed to the belief that light skin is superior to dark, then that same prejudice would likely apply to the Black community in the U.S. Some experts have drawn parallels between the Black community in America and the Dalit community in India, suggesting Indians who prescribe to caste preference may see the Black community as Dalits or an underclass unworthy of support. This theory is strengthened by the fact that many of the immigrants who came from South Asia in the 1960s were skilled and educated workers and were likely from higher castes in South Asia.[5]

Though the exact roots for anti-Black sentiment in South Asian culture may be hard to elucidate, it's not a far stretch to suggest that its hierarchical caste system, which is deeply intertwined with the damaging penchant for colorism, plays a role in how South Asians view Black people in America.

This ability to dehumanize entire groups of people is powerful and damaging. The social hierarchies that determine how South Asian culture categorizes people makes it easier for members of the South Asian diaspora to dehumanize people based on their perceived caste status. If caste preference influences skin tone preference, this caste-based colorism can possibly be extrapolated on how the South Asian community perceives the Black community.

Finally, many immigrants coming from Asia to the United States relied on the media to learn more about American culture—as well as the cultures of other minorities in their new country. Many of the portrayals dehumanized Black people,

---

5. Education was a privilege held predominantly by those with higher caste status in South Asia. The discrepancies in wealth in South Asia are huge. Wealth is predominantly held by those with higher caste status, and access to education is typically reserved for those with the privilege of higher caste status.

focusing on crime and poverty rates in struggling neighborhoods that were predominantly Black. Our parents and grandparents internalized these messages propagated from the media, compounding whatever caste-based colorism they brought to America with them.

CHAPTER 12

The Media's Influence on Immigrants

———

As I spoke to friends and acquaintances from both the South Asian community specifically and the Asian community more broadly, I noticed a trend that many of our parents used the news media as a source of knowledge and education as they learned about life in America.

My mother, who spent most of her life in England until she moved to America to marry my father at the age of twenty-one, often told me she and my grandparents would spend their evenings watching the news together.

"I did notice when I came to America that the Black people here seemed different," she told me when I asked her why she believed in the negatives stereotypes our community had of Black people.

"How so?" I asked.

"Well, to be honest, other than my Black field consultant, the only exposure I had to Black people was through what the media showed me. And, on the news, all the Black people I saw were gangbangers and thugs. They were very rarely exposed as being good people. They seemed violent, angry, and involved with drugs. You know, there were always stories involving drugs and violence, so that's what I knew about Black people in America. It was all from the news."

My mum paused for a moment, and then continued.

"I had very limited exposure to Black culture. I just thought the Black people in America were different from the ones I knew in England. So, in my mind, it was a cultural thing, not so much a race thing. I didn't have negative opinions about the Black people in England."

"But you did about the ones in America?" I clarified.

"Well, from what I saw on the news, yes. They just seemed more violent."

I thought of my friend Mark, a young man who was born in California to Korean immigrants. He had told me something similar about his parents absorbing the narrative created around the Black community by American media. I share his story because, though this book focuses on the South Asian community primarily, it's useful to see similarities in other Asian cultures as well.

"My dad, [when I was] growing up, he would make generalizations about the Black community. And then I would say, 'What about my best friend? He's Black.' And my dad would reply, 'Well, not him, obviously. He's different.'"

Mark explained, "The generalizations my parents had were very much media-inspired, and they were pretty negative. They'd say things like, 'Be careful going down the street, a Black person might rob you or hurt you,' or something like that. They'd mention that all the homeless people they'd see in LA were Black, so they would think Black people in general were homeless. Or that they're generally committing crimes, or they were violent. A lot of things came from the news. My parents were heavy news watchers growing up. And when the Rodney King verdict and the subsequent riots happened, my parents experienced all of that. The media would say that Black people were looting hardworking Korean stores, and my parents saw all that. So that divide between the Korean and Black communities, it got even bigger."

Mark also mentioned something that resonated with me. his family used the Korean word for "dirt" to describe his Ethiopian friend. It was not done out of malice. It was simply the word used to describe Black people in the Korean language. Like in the Punjabi language, there didn't seem to be a specific word for Black people.

Mark did clarify that his family didn't just make generalizations about Black people. "There were generalizations about the Chinese community. There were generalizations about the Japanese, which you know there's a long history there between Japanese and Korean communities. There weren't too many generalizations about white people, though. It was just like, oh, 'White people are white people.' That was the extent of that."

What's interesting, though, is Mark's parents *learned* about Black culture, and as a result formed their opinions about the Black community, from the media, in the same way my own mother learned about Black culture. Unfortunately, the media has a long history of portraying the Black community unfavorably and with prejudice, particularly during the twentieth century. In fact, media bias is still an issue today (Staples 2021).

A study conducted between 2015 and 2016 explored the portrayal of the Black community in the media. The researchers analyzed eight hundred news stories across multiple networks and newspaper outlets (including the *Washington Post*,

USA Today, the *New York Times*, and *Wall Street Journal*). Researchers found the media overwhelmingly portrayed families living in poverty as Black families (versus white) and exaggerated the proportion of Black families receiving welfare. The study also found news and opinion media overrepresented Black people as criminals while underrepresenting white people as criminals (Rodgers and Robinson 2017).

This study shows that the media creates a specific image of the Black community as one typified by poverty and crime. This is the same image the media offered to our parents and grandparents when they came to this country. It is the image our South Asian community has internalized.

Mark and I weren't the only ones to realize the impact of media on our parent's perception of Black people.

Hazeem, an acquaintance born in Pakistan but who grew up in America, shared that his parents, like ours, were influenced by the media.

"I knew my parents had certain biases. It seemed to be such a part of the background noise of the entire world, the kind of racism they were exhibiting. You know, stuff like associating Black with being more violent or [being] gang members. I know that that was a big concern because there were some bad things that happened in our neighborhood when I was growing up, and the people who were involved were Black. It seemed to fit into this narrative that the media would show them in general, and we didn't get a whole lot to counter it. And some of the kids in school, sometimes they themselves would exhibit part of the stereotypes my parents saw in the news."

My friend Riz, whose family originated from Bangladesh, also found that her parents learned through the news outlets when the family immigrated to America.

When I was discussing my book with Riz, I was sharing the conversation I had with my mother about her learned perceptions about Black people.

"My parents were the same way," Riz said.

"I came to America when I was ten years old," Riz explained. "My parents worked so hard to assimilate, and so much of what they learned about race was absolutely from the media. It was also a lot from members of their community that were in America—from the other aunties and uncles who they affiliated with, who have been here for decades, who themselves probably also learned it from the media."

"And it was a narrative they were fed every time they saw a robbery or something on the news," she continued. "The way they depicted a Black man versus the way they would depict the robbery had it been a white man was very different. And we know these biases. We know now that they're perpetual. And so that fed into my parents' minds and into our communities' minds, and it wasn't just about Black folks. It was also with the Latinx community. So, much was really influenced by the media. That is a big source of the anti-Blackness for the Bangladeshi community."

The reality is how we view the world is deeply impacted by the narratives we are taught by our parents and families. The fact that our parents themselves were taught a particular narrative about Black people perpetuated a cycle of anti-Black prejudice and racism.

So much so that, as South Asians, being romantically involved with a Black person isn't even an option for many of us.

In fact, in October 2022, during the final stages of revising this book, Mel and I bumped into a Black and Indian couple during an outing. The woman, Rani, was a Punjabi American woman and her partner, Leon, was a Liberian American man.

"Her father offered me a large sum of money to leave her," Leon told us. "He didn't want his daughter to be with a Black man."

Leon wasn't the first person I'd met who shared a story like this. My friend Chris, a Jamaican man who came to America when he was eighteen, told me his ex-girlfriend's Indian father purchased her a home and expensive car in exchange for her agreement to end her relationship with Chris. He did not want a Black man in the family. Chris's ex-girlfriend agreed to the exchange.

For some South Asians, being in a relationship with a Black person isn't even considered a remote possibility. My acquaintance Hazeem discussed this about his Pakistani community.

"What would your parents do if your sister came home with a Black guy?" I asked him. His younger sister had just started dating.

"Honestly, I have no idea. Even the thought of it is bizarre. It's a great question, though, because there were some girls in our community who would come home with white guys. When stuff like that happened, it would be almost a joke. Like, we'd say 'Oh, look at that family, look what they have to deal with.' But bringing home a Black guy is unexpected to such a degree that a part of me is curious to see what *would* happen. It'd just be such a shock, which I think in itself speaks volumes because it's so unthinkable. Dealing with a white guy would be so bad, but dealing with a Black guy? It would just be considered such a bizarre thing to do."

"So Black people don't even register as an option for partnership?" I asked him.

Hazeem thought for a moment.

"Yeah," he said finally. "I think there's this idea that with white people, there's an appeal to them. They're lighter skinned. They're wealthier, right? They have this aura in the minds of people who immigrated here that they are what you aspire to, while maintaining your own cultural values. You want that wealth, that status of being white, but without having sold out, so to speak. Being white is aspirational."

Hazeem's words were also, as discussed in a previous chapter, at the core of why many South Asian immigrants fed into the model minority myth. Assimilating was a way to become "more white," and therefore "less inferior." And one of the most effective ways to become "more white" was to separate themselves from the Black community, which contributed to the anti-Blackness within the South Asian diaspora.

Anti-Blackness is Global

Though I've focused predominantly on anti-Blackness in the United States, it's still important to note that anti-Blackness is prevalent in the larger South Asian diaspora.

Black people weren't just prohibited as romantic partners or spouses in America. One of my colleagues, Sarika, was born and raised in Australia to Sri Lankan parents.

"We have a policy in our family," Sarika told me over dinner. "No ATMs."

I looked at her in confusion. "What does banking have to do with any of this?"

She laughed.

"No Africans, Tamils, or Muslims," Sarika explained. "No ATMs. It was just a rule. We didn't question it. Is it a problem? Sure. Do I think it'll change anytime soon? I don't know. But I hope so."

Though I knew South Asian culture in America was prejudiced against Black people, I don't think I realized just how truly pervasive it was outside of America.

A Bengali woman I met on social media, Tanya, shared a similar "off-limits" policy in her community when she was growing up in Toronto. Tanya owns and operates a business called Blindian Bliss, a life coaching program that helps Black and South Asian women navigate Blindian (Black + Indian) relationships.

During our call, Tanya described her Bengali community in Toronto, Canada.

"There's a huge Indian population in Toronto," she explained. "Most of my friends who were Indian were dating other Indian guys. One degree outside of it being acceptable to date at all (because you weren't even supposed to be dating at this point) was dating a white guy. But Black men were completely off the table. Like, that wasn't even a conversation. It just wasn't a thing, but it wasn't something anybody thought about or talked about. It wasn't actually expressed."

She elaborated, "We began to see interracial white marriages. And then also Muslim-Hindu marriages, which was a pretty big deal back then. Then I realized that being with a Black man still wasn't acceptable."

Though she lived in Canada, Tanya also noted the impact the media had on her community's perception of Black people in Canada.

"I think the news was probably a big part of it. Like, even though our communities may have been integrated in Canada, especially in Toronto, there was still definitely a bias against Black people when it came to poverty and crime, when it came to Black men and their families, you know. You're still seeing a lot of those narratives and stories that reinforce those biases. So I think that a lot of time when people aren't informed, they buy into that."

The media's power can be seen in the way it shaped an entire generation of South Asians' perception of the Black community. It compounded the colorism and inherent anti-Blackness our culture already exhibited in a way we are still trying to dismantle today.

The media didn't just influence my parents' and grandparents' generations of South Asian immigrants, however. The media also strongly influenced South Asian youths, who have historically exploited Black culture for their amusement, entertainment, and popularity currency.

It's not uncommon to hear young South Asian men toss anti-Black racial slurs at each other, to speak in Blaccent (which is the accent used by non-Black people to imitate Black people), and to adopt Black mannerisms. These aspects of Black culture are popular amongst not only South Asian youth but also South Asian celebrities. From Lilly Singh (a famous YouTuber who routinely adopts Black mannerism and hairstyles when it suits her) to NAV (a rapper-producer from Toronto who openly uses the "n" word in his music), South Asian celebrities routinely appropriate and exploit Black culture in their content and music.

Even Ravi, despite the anti-Black prejudice he displayed, loved listening to rap music and occasionally spoke in Blaccent.

Evidently, Black culture is "cool" enough to emulate and commodify for these South Asians, but it can be removed from their identity when they need to be separated from the Black experience. They want to benefit from being "Black and cool" without living in this world as an actual Black person—and without treating Black people as equals.

Part 5

CHAPTER 13

"Your Baby Won't Be Black"

As I wrote this book, I began to talk openly about my writing and learning journey with friends. I frequently shared the experience of writing this book with loved ones, as I wanted to engage in dialogue with those in my life and explore their thoughts and perspectives on what I was learning.

In August 2021 I was at brunch with two people I met through Mel. They are also a biracial couple comprised of a Black woman and a white man. The woman, Valerie, is an insightful woman with an open mind and a passion for educating others and engaging in dynamic conversation. We've discussed controversial topics many times, and during this particular meal she said something that struck me.

The topic of Kamala Harris came up when we were talking about different parenting methods and how they could impact the development of a biracial child. The conversation was interwoven with some commentary on politics, and I referred to Kamala Harris as the first Black vice president.

"Kamala Harris is *not* Black," Valerie said passionately. "Black people don't consider her Black." She continued to take bites of her food and carried on the conversation about different parenting ideologies.

I couldn't focus on what she was saying because I felt so confused about her words about Kamala Harris. Kamala Harris referred to herself as a Black woman. How could she not be Black? I waited until Valerie finished a sentence and then broke in.

"Actually, can you go back to what you said about Kamala Harris not being Black?" I asked. "Isn't she considered to be the first female, first Black, and first South Asian vice president in U.S. History? Also… will my baby not be considered Black?"

"Kamala Harris is as Black as Barack Obama is Black," Val responded by way of explanation (which didn't feel like an explanation to me at all). She sat up straighter and leaned forward as she chewed. "And I'd argue that your kid won't be Black, no. I would never consider the color green as 'blue' nor gray as 'black.' Both colors have their own uniqueness and are given respective names to identify with. I believe the same to be true with biracial people. A biracial person's experience is very different than that of Black people. This doesn't mean they won't experience racism or discrimination, but they'll experience it in a manner not equivalent to that of Black people."

"So where do biracial people fit in then?" I asked. "Where will our child find community, if you're saying our biracial child won't be Black? We already know the Indian community is anti-Black."

Val's response was cut off when the waiter came and brought us the check, and Val's husband began talking to her. Distracted, Val didn't elaborate. Brunch was coming to an end, and I decided not to push it. My belly was huge, and my back hurt. I felt emotionally sensitive and hormonal—not a good combination for a discussion on race and politics.

Later that day, her words still ate at me. As I mulled over our conversation, I flashed back to a therapy session I had eighteen months earlier, before Mel and I began to seriously consider having children together. I'd sought the counsel of a Black male therapist who had worked with individuals with backgrounds similar to Mel's.

At that point in our relationship, I needed help understanding Mel. I was struggling to come to grips with certain elements of his past he'd shared with me. Our backgrounds were so different, and we were fighting often because I couldn't understand how the man I was in love with would have done and experienced some of the things my partner had done and experienced in his youth.

The therapist was an incredibly tall, broad-shouldered man named Jeffrey. Jeffrey was soft-spoken and had kind eyes. His patient demeanor almost felt like a hug. Calmness emanated from him, and his patience was the inherent and genuine kind, not simply the kind of patience therapists reserved for their clients.

The flecks of gray in his close-cropped hair made the darkness of his skin seem deeper and richer, and his brown eyes watched me intently. He always leaned back in his chair as I spoke, giving me space to explore my own insecurities and the disbeliefs I struggled with as I learned to navigate the complexities of my biracial, bicultural relationship.

"I'm scared that if I have a family with this man, and our relationship ends, my Indian community will ostracize me. It's one thing to date a Black man. It's an entirely different level to have children with one."

Jeffrey looked at me thoughtfully. He hesitated before responding, "Your fears are valid. Your community may shun you if you have children with this man and your relationship doesn't last. But that doesn't mean every person in your community will ostracize you. I do want to ask you something, though. Do you realize the world won't see your child as Indian? Your child, in the eyes of society today, will be considered Black."

I shook my head. "No, our children will be half Punjabi, half Black."

Jeffrey responded quietly, "Yes, they will be. But they will be widely perceived as Black by the outside world. They will struggle in a way you haven't struggled."

My eyes burned, and I began to cry. I was overwhelmed, grappling with how to process this information, wiping away snot and tears as I thought about Jeffrey's words.

Eighteen months later, I sat snuggled next to Mel, hours after our brunch with Valerie and her husband. Jeffrey told me if I had a baby with Mel our child would be seen as Black by the world. Why did Val tell me our baby wouldn't be Black?

"I'm still really confused by what Valerie said at breakfast today," I told Mel, as he nuzzled my neck and moved his hand over my growing belly. "If our kid won't be considered fully Indian and they won't be considered Black… where will they fit in?"

Mel responded without hesitation. "Val doesn't get to tell us what our kid is or isn't. She's one person with an opinion. Don't let it get to you."

I sat up and moved away from him, turning to face him (no easy feat with a belly the size of a soccer ball).

"I'm serious, though. What did she mean, our baby won't be Black? You're Black. Doesn't it bother you that your Black friend won't consider your child a member of your Black community?"

He thought about my question for a moment before meeting my eyes and saying, as if his words were the most obvious things in the world, "We don't need to explain to anyone that our baby is Black enough to be considered 'Black.' And I don't need anyone to give me permission for anything. I don't need Valerie's blessing for my kid to be Black. I'm Black. My baby is Black. Period."

Mel thought the entire conversation was absurd. He was in no way interested in allowing anyone to tell us who our child would or would not be. To him, our child would be Black. And our child would be Indian. They would also be American. Our child would hold all these identities, and none of them canceled the other out.

And I, a woman who is decidedly not Black, didn't know how to process any of it.

Why was I so agitated by Valerie's comment?

As I wrote this book, I explored my obsession with this particular topic of identity. My obsession was rooted in the fact that the question of identity is one that has plagued me since I was a child. I was a brown girl growing up in a predominantly white world. I was never "white" enough to truly fit in within the white world. But I was never really "Indian" enough to truly fit in with my Punjabi world.

My skin color, my heritage, is inescapable. And it is very much tied into my concept of "identity." Every time I look in the mirror, I see the features of my Punjabi blood. My appearance is an inexorable part of who I am, and the society I grew up in treated me differently because of it. I have always battled a deep-rooted, pervasive sense of discomfort when it came to my place in the world.

I've battled these feelings since my childhood. Would my child struggle with this too? Would this struggle be worse for them? What will it be like for my child, if their "otherness" was already being highlighted before they were even born?

My child would look like me. But my child would also look like Mel. And the world Mel grew up in treated him harshly, and sometimes violently, for how he looks.

Our physical appearance—our skin color—impacted how the world treated us both. And, as children, it affected how we valued ourselves in society.

But that society has changed in the last twenty years. There are more people of color in this country now than there have ever been. But I still have painful scars that remind me of how awful it feels when you cannot find your footing in any world.

I wrestle with questions some might find offensive, but whether or not they are offensive, they are thoughts that still come up. What if my child presents very strongly as Black? Will the world treat them with the same animosity it showed Mel? The same violence and anger? Will they have a higher chance of being hurt?

Every day, I read stories about Black people being targeted. In the early stages of writing this book, I read an article that discussed a white officer in Indianapolis handcuffing a Black man on the ground and kicking his face (Vera and Alonso 2021). The morning I wrote this chapter, I read an article of a Black woman being bullied and assaulted by three young white boys and, after stumbling home, being stopped by a police officer. Because she wouldn't stop to talk to him and tried to continue to walk home, he dragged her to the ground and wrestled her, smashing her head into the pavement (Webster 2021).

In 2020, when racial tension in this country hit a peak, nooses were found in Las Vegas, Oregon, Portland, Nebraska, and Delaware. Five Black men were found hanging from trees in California, New York, Texas, and New Jersey. Local authorities ruled these hangings as suicides, despite protests and pleas from the public to further investigate the hangings as possible hate crimes (Philimon 2020).

In May 2022, a white man targeted a grocery store in a predominantly Black neighborhood in Buffalo, New York. The shooter had written a manifesto on white supremacy and was fueled with hatred for the Black community. He killed ten people and injured more. He attacked these people because they were Black (Morrison 2022). He decided their lives, because of their skin color, had no value and needed to end.

In the year it took me to write this book, crimes against the Black community have risen. In 2020 the FBI reported the highest number of hate crimes since 2008, with more than 50 percent of these hate crimes targeted at Black people. Stories of violence against Black people have increased since the summer of 2020. Officials speculated that the social justice movement spurred by the murder of George Floyd brought more attention and anger toward the Black community by people who already had preexisting inclinations for anti-Blackness (Equal Justice Initiative 2021).

The week before I submitted my revised manuscript to my publisher, news broke that the president of the Los Angeles City Council was caught on tape making racist remarks about a young Black boy, referring to him as a monkey and suggesting he needed a beating (Riddle 2022).

As I read the headlines and pay attention to the events within my country, I can't help but ask: Will it be better by the time my child is grown?

How do I prepare them for a world that can be so cruel? And how can I prepare them for anti-Blackness, when I am not Black myself?

I also find myself thinking, *Would I think so much about this if I wasn't with a Black man? If I wasn't carrying his child? If the answer is 'no,' what kind of person does that make me?*

The reality is racial tension continues to be a pervasive reality in this country, and If I still struggle with my own sense of identity (particularly after my divorce, when I have few opportunities to speak my native tongue and rarely cook the Punjabi foods of my childhood), how can I raise a child who has a strong sense of identity?

I don't think I will know the answer to that question for a few decades at least, when my child is grown and moving through the world on their own.

What I do know is there is no person better suited to me than Mel, no person who could better help me navigate the anxieties I grappled with during my pregnancy.

When I was in my second trimester, I found out one of my estranged cousins, who had married a white man, was pregnant. I shared the news with a family friend, Nikunj. Nikunj chuckled when I told him.

"Now we have a half-white baby on the way. So you'll have a half-Black baby, she'll have a half-white baby. Maybe someone else in the family will give us a fully brown baby."

I forced myself to laugh, even though I felt my brow furrow. Was my baby not good enough because it wasn't fully brown? Did he see a need for a fully brown baby? I knew Nikunj had a politically incorrect sense of humor. Why was I taking this so personally?

Later that day, I told Mel about what Nikunj had said. "What did he mean?" I asked Mel, following him around the condo like a puppy while he gathered up random socks and pieces of paper he'd thrown here and there during his busy week.

"Babe, don't overthink it," he said. "Nik was just kidding around. He didn't mean anything by it." He walked down the stairs, and I followed closely on his heels.

"No," I insisted, "why would he even say it then? Does he think our baby isn't as desirable as a fully Indian baby?" Though I didn't typically invalidate my own feelings during my pregnancy by blaming them on hormones, I felt irrationally upset. My eyes watered, and my throat tightened with the intensity of my emotions.

Mel put his papers and empty water bottle down on the kitchen table and turned toward me, pulling me into his arms. "Babe, stop stressing. I know you're worried. You're going to be a great mother." He rested his chin on my head. "I think this book is making you overthink all these things. We are going to be great parents. Our kid is going to have a strong sense of value and self-love. I promise."

I began to cry, feeling ridiculous and emotional with my raging pregnancy hormones. "But where will they belong? Where will they fit in?"

"Here. With us. In this family," Mel said firmly.

And then (again, hugely pregnant and overwhelmed), I sniffled and said, "I don't know how to take care of Black hair. What if our baby has Black hair and I don't know how to take care of it? I can barely figure out how to take care of my own hair."

Mel laughed and kissed my forehead. "I'll teach you, and my mom will teach you. We're going to be great parents, babe. It's all going to be okay."

CHAPTER 14

Growth is Uncomfortable

My first corporate job after going to business school was at a large health care company. My manager at the time was a conservative white woman who lived in Massachusetts and had been vocal about her conservative political viewpoints.

"I'm not racist," she insisted one day, on a call during which she felt the need to vent about the Black Lives Matter protests. "I just don't think rioting is okay." Later in the conversation, she told me, "My sister-in-law won't talk to me because she says I'm racist for not supporting Colin Kaepernick. I think the whole kneeling during the national anthem is, quite frankly, absurd. But that doesn't make me racist."

I remember thinking, *Okay. So you don't support peaceful kneeling during sports events as a form of activism… but you also don't support marching or protesting. How do you think marginalized people should express their demands for change?*

To my shame, I did not ask her that. I simply listened and offered no pushback. This same manager, weeks later, made a snarky comment about a Black colleague's hair (the only Black employee in our department at the time). "Cassie has such a horrible attitude," my manager complained. "And don't even get me started on her hair. I don't know what she's thinking letting it look like that."

Cassie is a Black woman who wears her hair naturally. I knew her hair was a source of pride and it had taken years to get to the point where she was comfortable wearing it naturally in a corporate setting.

I was horrified by my manager's comment, but instead of calling her out on her inappropriate (and racist) comment, I quickly found a reason to end the call. My manager had gone out on a limb for me when she offered me this job. She had convinced *her* manager to bring me into the team because she saw my potential. I didn't know how to confront her anti-Blackness, since I had my job as a direct result of her generosity.

I share this story because I still feel guilt over how I did nothing when this manager ridiculed my colleague's natural hair. I feel shame that I allowed my manager to denigrate someone I respected, that I did nothing in response so I could maintain my own position at the proverbial table.

It is *hard* to speak up. It is *hard* to push back when anti-Blackness rears its head in more subtle ways.

Because anti-Black racism isn't always violence, hate, and intensity. It can be innocuous. It can be quiet. It can be casual conversation.

And when you encounter it in the workplace, it can be intimidating. Even encountering it amongst people you consider friends is intimidating.

A few months before completing my graduate program, I was at dinner with some friends from business school. One of my friends at the dinner was a highly educated young Korean

American woman named Grace. During our conversation, I told Grace that I drove up to Pleasanton, California, with Mel to explore the new city I had planned on moving to for my new job post-MBA. Pleasanton is a hub for those in the tech and health care industries, and it is considered a higher-income area.

I shared that Mel and I had seen a large number of people from Asian backgrounds everywhere we went but had seen only a small handful of Black people during our entire trip.

Grace listened, tilted her head, and replied, "Well, Black people only make up like 13 percent of the population, right? So doesn't it kind of make sense that you didn't really see a lot of Black people there?"

Her response confused me, and in the silence that followed as I tried to process what she meant, her boyfriend asked a follow-up question about my trip. The conversation veered off onto a different topic, and I decided to process my thoughts about Grace's response a little more before addressing what she'd said.

Later that night I still felt confused by her response and decided to reach out to talk about it more.

Hi, Grace, I texted. *Just wanted to follow up on a comment you made at dinner. The fact that Black people make up a little under 13 percent of the population isn't an adequate explanation for why there weren't many Black people up north. Asians make up less than 6 percent of the population, but there was an incredibly high number of Asians (and white people) concentrated in the area we visited. We have better access to opportunities that allow us to work in tech and corporate health care. The issue has to do with access and systemic oppression.*

Grace never responded to that message. In fact, when we met in person a month later at a graduation event, she avoided eye contact. We haven't really spoken much since that exchange.

But my interaction with Grace was a critical wake-up call for me. If someone as hyper-educated as Grace (the daughter of a prominent figure in academia) can have such a skewed perspective on the racial experience in America despite all the resources made available during the Black Lives Matter movement, how many other people continued to engage in tacit anti-Blackness?

Because, in my mind, attempting to justify inequities without addressing the realities of targeted oppression *is* anti-Blackness.

My interactions with both my manager and Grace were also red flags for me personally. At that time, I still struggled to immediately address problematic comments or behavior.

Speaking up and advocating doesn't come easy for everyone. I share this because it definitely didn't come easy for me. That does not mean, however, I was not capable of change.

Part of being a self-subscribed member of the model minority is that I am a people pleaser. I don't like to cause problems, I don't like to displease people, and I definitely don't want people to not like me.

That's part of the problem though. That is how white supremacy and anti-Black racism continue to flourish: because we are afraid to ruffle feathers by speaking OUT. We are afraid to upset people, to push back against our elders, our community, our managers, our friends, our neighbors, and our acquaintances.

It's easier to stay quiet. It's easier not to speak up. It's easier not to push back.

But silence is tacit consent to the status quo, and the status quo is, quite frankly, unacceptable. Because the status quo is a society that remains rife with inequity, prejudice, and ignorance. Silence is a contribution to the problem.

You cannot be anti-racist and be silent. Silence and anti-racism oppose each other.

And being in a relationship with a Black person or having Black friends does not automatically make a person anti-racist. Every time someone said something problematic and I did not call them out on it, I was part of the problem. My silence in the face of anti-Blackness actually *contributed* to the propagation of anti-Blackness around me.

I mentioned before that anti-Blackness isn't always overt. It's not always an "in-your-face" sticker people wear plastered on their foreheads. I was an example of this. The thoughts and experiences I shared from my past, from my relationship with Ravi and my community, are all examples of complicity in anti-Black racism. But I was a "good person." We are all "good people."

That's why certain forms of anti-Blackness are so insidious. They fly under the radar, or as is the case with the South Asian community, are such an ingrained part of our existence that they don't even register to us unless they're pointed out.

And *that* is why I share my story: to show you that if I can challenge myself, if I can come from a culture that is both overtly and covertly anti-Black and actively push back against it, so can you. My journey toward growth has definitely been uncomfortable. Facing the parts of yourself that are lacking, that are less than savory, is never easy. But it's only by admitting to their existence, by acknowledging these aspects of ourselves, that we can begin dismantling them and rebuilding ourselves into the type of people we want to be.

It doesn't take a lot either. It literally just starts with conversations, with self-reflection, and with self-acknowledgement.

By first acknowledging your own contribution to the problem, you can begin untangling yourself from the narratives you've consumed and internalized.

And from there, you can begin engaging in conversations with others in your life: your friends, cousins, parents, and grandparents.

Because that's where we can all start to elicit change: through conversations with loved ones.

Engaging in these types of conversations with my parents is not easy. In the past they involved tears and feelings of frustration, but, with persistence, I have noticed in recent years that these conversations typically result in a positive resolution and a deeper connection between myself and my parents.

My relationship with my parents, and their acceptance of Mel as my life partner, is the by-product of concerted effort from all parties involved. I had to initiate the conversations. I had to explain to them why certain views and beliefs were rooted in prejudice, why certain jokes are problematic. I had to meet them where they were and understand what their capacity was at any given point. I had to actively learn where their beliefs came from. I had to explore their fears to truly understand them.

What's more, I had to be willing to displease them, to upset them. Coming from a culture where obedience is a virtue, learning to sit in the discomfort of displeasing my parents was incredibly challenging—so much so that I spent the first twenty-seven years of my life marching to the beat of *their* drum instead of honoring my own.

But the people my parents are today are hardly recognizable from the people they were fifteen years ago. I'd even go so far as to say they are unrecognizable from the people they were six years ago, when I left my marriage.

They have challenged their perspective on race. They have acknowledged their prejudicial views.

When I asked him if he truly accepted my relationship with Mel, my father said, "If you'd asked me ten years ago, I would have said no. But I'm a different person now. Who cares what a person's skin color is. What their religion is. Are they a good person? Do they respect you? Do they love you and care for you and provide for you? I love Mel! I used to be homophobic, for God's sake. But I'm a different person now. I thank God for showing me this path, and now my focus is to stay on this path."

"You know I may share some of the painful things the family has said and done in the past, right? In my book?" I asked him one afternoon as I was revising my manuscript.

My father looked at me, his eyes calm, and he nodded. "Good," he said. "You should share them." I'd be lying if I said a feeling of relief didn't wash over me at his acceptance.

CHAPTER 15

Conversations with Loved Ones

Despite the evolution they've undergone, the summer of 2020 was still rife with challenging lessons for my parents. Explaining to them that targeted violence toward Black people was prevalent in America also involved explaining the history of Black oppression in America. It involved calling out our own community's history of anti-Blackness.

Around the country, younger generations of Asian Americans were educating their parents and grandparents in the same way. We, as a community, began challenging the myth of the model minority.

And thankfully, many people in my circle found their elders were open to shifting their belief systems. My friend Mark is one of them.

He recounted his experience of speaking to his parents about the Black Lives Matter protests.

Referring to his parents, Mark said, "I told them, 'The Black community is oppressed. We've been oppressed as Koreans. We've experienced racism, so we should support other communities that are also experiencing discrimination.' And I think putting things in that light made them realize that everything is nuanced. And I've noticed my parents no longer refer to Black people using the Korean word for dirt anymore."

Mark also explained, "During the height of the anti-Asian sentiment in 2021, my mother had been given this emergency kit that was made for older Asian people. It was written in Korean. It had information on what to do if you were assaulted or harassed and had other resources you could refer to if you needed help. And it had a whistle. So she had this kit with her, and she told me that she was running an errand. She'd parked her car and was walking, and she noticed somebody behind her who seemed to be following her. She was scared because of all the anti-Asian hate going around. She decided to take a different route because her original plan was to go down this alleyway. But she thought that was too dangerous. She wanted to go somewhere very public, so she went into a restaurant and pretended to order something just because she knew there were cameras and other people there, and she'd feel safer."

My heart hurt as I listened to Mark speak. During Donald Trump's presidency, the country saw a surge in anti-Asian violence resulting from careless comments made by Trump regarding COVID-19 and China. To the dismay of most of the country, older Asian individuals in particular had been the targets of some horrific acts of violence.

Mark continued, "And I remember she was telling me all this, and she said, 'The guy who was walking behind me... I noticed he was Black. And I remember you told me not to judge somebody just because of their skin color. So I told myself not to think that this man was following me just because he is Black.' She stopped to make that distinction. She realized 'oh, he's not scaring me because he's Black, that has nothing to do with it. I'm scared because there's a lot of anti-Asian hate, not because of the color of his skin.' So she took that moment to assess why she felt nervous."

The fact that Mark's mother made an effort to identify the root cause of her fear is critical. It demonstrates that people, no matter their age or generation, are capable of change.

Mark was one of many people I know who actively engaged in dialogue with their parents during the Black Lives Matter protests. Hazeem, my Pakistani acquaintance who shared the impact of the media on his parents, also told me about the work his mother has done to understand the race-fueled politics depicted in the media. Hazeem's mother worked in public schools and was exposed to Black people on a daily basis because many of the teachers and students she worked with were Black. Even she felt the bias in the media regarding how Black people were portrayed during the race protests in 2020.

"My mom had questions about what it meant to defund the police and about why there was so much violence during the looting and riots. I didn't ever make her feel bad when she talked to me about some of the things she thought. And I'll give her this much: She did put in the work to understand it all. It wasn't easy, given that so many of the rioters were portrayed as violent looters. But she worked to understand what was really going on."

Even older generations are capable of shifting their paradigms. Cultures are carried by people. If people can change, so too can culture. And our culture of anti-Blackness *can* be slowly dismantled if enough of us educate our loved ones and push back on the value systems we've inherited.

It will not happen overnight. It will not happen in one conversation, and it may not happen for years or even in one lifetime. But shifting the perspectives our elders carry *is* possible.

My friend Riz hopes to one day change how her parents see the world. One of our conversations was a discussion on the impact of the Black Lives Matter protests on our parents' understanding of race in America.

"How did you handle conversations about race during the 2020 protests?" I asked her.

Riz mulled over my question before answering. "My brother and sister-in-law have the same views as me," she said. "They're more educated on the subject and feel strongly that there are systems in place targeting people of color. The conversations with my parents are certainly much harder. The conversations really started with voting. They're both citizens, but my mother hadn't voted in the 2016 election, which blew my mind. I was like, okay, do you understand who is currently the president of this country and why? Do you know how much damage this one man has done in four years, damage we're going to be trying to unlearn and undo over the next one hundred years? So that's how a lot of the conversation started after George Floyd's murder. It was a lot of 'you need to get to the polls for the 2020 election, and you have to vote. This is why you have to vote' and it led to these conversations of 'do you understand why there are protests happening?'"

I listened intently, nodding my head as she spoke. She paused for a moment, and I asked, "What did they say when you asked them those types of questions?"

Riz responded, "My parents, even to this day, haven't made the connection between the things you're writing about with regards to colorism or them feeling like they have to assimilate into American culture in order to succeed and survive… they haven't made the connection of how all that has fed into the anti-Blackness in our community. So I started with something tangible, which was at least getting them to vote. That's a start."

I could hear frustration in her voice, and I understood it. It is hard to see the people you love cling so stubbornly to myopia. And it's uncomfortable to know that people you care so deeply about can hold onto such problematic views.

But clichés can help drive home a point, and my favorite is: nothing worth doing comes easy.

How Do You Have These Conversations?

There are innumerable articles and resources available to help members of the Asian American community (and even the South Asian American community specifically) engage in anti-racism work. You can find examples of these resources online and at the end of this book.

At a high level, though, the conversations we need to have with our loved ones must include empathy for the journeys our loved ones have undergone as members of marginalized communities themselves.

It's also important to remember these conversations don't just need to happen once or twice. They should be part of an evergreen dialogue and continuous process of learning. For instance, my parents and brothers fully embraced Mel into the family when they realized how serious our relationship was. They saw him as a son and brother, respectively, and they enjoyed learning about Black culture through him. However, loving Mel didn't erase their anti-Black prejudice. Their love and acceptance of one Black man was not automatically extrapolated onto the entire Black community.

They still harbored ignorance and prejudice. They still had much to learn (just as I, even after writing this book, still have much to learn). For that reason, conversations on anti-Blackness should be ongoing.

What's more, we must also learn to engage with our elders and modulate our own frustrations during the conversation. There have been times when I felt I was talking to a wall, where nothing I was saying was being heard or received. If you've experienced situations like this, losing your temper or ending a conversation out of anger or frustration isn't productive. Remain calm. Take a breath. Allow the conversation to come to a resolution, and if it ends abruptly, take initiative to let the other person know that the lines of communication remain open.

I've said it many times: This work is hard. Be ready to feel tired. These conversations are exhausting, and it's especially challenging to feel motivated to have them when you know your loved ones will argue or disagree with you.

Anti-Blackness in the South Asian community has generations and generations of longevity. It will not be dismantled in a day, month, or year. You have to think of the long game. Do not give up after one or two or three conversations, and do not give up if your loved ones become upset.

It is hard to undo a lifetime of conditioning in a short period of time.

As a community, we must normalize having challenging conversations with our family. We must normalize upsetting our parents with our personal growth and development. We must normalize not being the "obedient" children they want us to be.

We must sit in the discomfort of displeasing our elders, of angering them.

If we are afraid to do the work at *home*, to engage with our own families, then everything else we do outside is performative.

And I do want to acknowledge that there are some individuals who will prove supremely difficult, some may even stay insufferably inflexible in their mindset. Some individuals who hold prejudiced viewpoints may believe in conspiracy theories or be out of touch with reality. I acknowledge these people may seem impossible to speak to, and in some cases they may be.

I used to think there was no point in wasting my time talking to people like this, until I realized I used to be one of them. I was a person who was so deeply self-righteous in her narrow-mindedness that I would even pull on my academic accolades to defend my positions. And it was only because people were patient with me and persistently poked holes in my beliefs that I changed.

No matter how intimidating or tiring it seems, we as a community have a moral imperative to discuss anti-Black racism. If we do not, any time we become upset when someone treats *us* with racism, we become hypocrites.

Some Tactical Advice

My biggest mistake when it came to engaging in challenging conversations with loved ones was assuming they'd be ready to jump in right away to face the alarming facts and statistics about anti-Blackness in America. I wanted to bring all my facts and knowledge to the table and present it to them, served on a metaphorical silver platter.

"Here," I wanted to say. "Look at all this information. Read it. Learn it. Know it. Change!"

That's not how these types of conversations work. I had to take a step back and learn how to communicate with my loved ones at a baseline first. I had to meet them where they were and understand their individual capacity, and then be more tactical with my approach.

For me, one of the first conversations I had with my mother involved me telling her about my day and sharing a story about me watching a documentary with Mel (13th on Netflix).

"It was a great movie," I told her. "I grew up thinking Black people were responsible for their own issues. I realize now there's a lot more to the story. Is it okay if I tell you about it?"

When you're armed with knowledge and passion, it's easy to run into a conversation with your metaphorical guns blazing, but that is a recipe for disaster. One thing I have noticed in both my own family as well as in other families is a reactive defensiveness when discussing racism. People resist discomfort, and having a flashlight spotlighting areas where they aren't their best selves is really uncomfortable. Also, many people don't like to admit they don't know something. It is for this reason that, during these types of conversations, I usually share my own blind spots and things I didn't know until someone educated *me*.

Approaching conversations on anti-Blackness with an energy of neutrality is key. People are less likely to listen to you if they feel attacked or feel you have become confrontational. And when *you* feel your loved one has become confrontational, it is crucial you remain calm. The line of communication should always stay open. The people you are talking to need to feel safe talking to you, otherwise they will build up walls of resistance and defensiveness. Change will never happen if those lines of communication are temperamental or unreliable.

Further, there's different avenues to approach these conversations. Whether it's a documentary you've watched, a news article you've read, a book you're enjoying, an experience with a colleague at work, or a conversation trending on social media: there's no end to the different ways you can bring up conversations about anti-Blackness with your loved ones. And, if approaching the topic head-on is intimidating, consider discussing different issues mentioned in this book: the model minority myth, colorism in our community, diversification and representation in movies and shows, or even interactions with other family members.

Another critical point is to actually *listen* to your loved one. So often we listen to respond versus listening to actually process and comprehend what the other person is saying. When we approach these conversations from a place of self-righteousness, it shifts how we show up in the conversation.

Let go of your expectations of your loved ones and simply engage. Listen. Offer insight. Ask questions. Show curiosity—you are talking to this person or these people because you care enough about them to want them to shift their perspective. If you truly want this person to change, and you truly want to maintain a relationship with them, you must be curious.

My Request of My Readers

As you process the information presented in this book, my "ask" of my readers is simple.

I am not asking you to grab a picket sign and go into the streets and protest. I am not asking you to donate money or sign a petition or become a public activist. I am not asking you to sever ties with anyone, to turn your life upside down, or to grab a megaphone and decry every anti-Black belief our community holds.

I am simply asking you to look at your personal sphere of influence, at the people in your life who you know you can impact, and to talk to them.

And sure, it may be that some members in your sphere of influence won't change. I'm not saying all it takes to dismantle anti-Blackness is talking about it and bringing it up. But you have to start somewhere. And there's no anti-racist tool that is more accessible, more affordable, and more actionable than a conversation.

A Word (or, Words) on Ravi

As I wrote this book, I struggled with the image of Ravi I portrayed to the world. He is a big part of my story because he was a big part of my life. He was a big part of me. Ravi was a critical presence during eight of the most formative years of my life.

When I first met Mel, I was still grieving the end of my marriage to Ravi, even though it had been years since our divorce.

Ravi was my first love and, aside for Mel, I have never loved another person with the depth and passion that I loved Ravi. Even now, after everything I've learned and experienced since leaving him, I truly believe his anti-Black prejudice and ignorance was a by-product of our community's influence rather than a reflection of his innate personal character. He, like most of us, was a by-product of his upbringing, of his culture.

Of my culture.

Of our culture.

I have kept accounts of our relationship high level, as I do not want to detract from the purpose of this book.

I also shied away from sharing much about our story because, truthfully, I needed to block myself off from the ache I felt in sharing the less-than-flattering aspects of what he represented about our culture.

The truth is I would not have married Ravi if I did not love him. He was my best friend for almost eight years. We chased sunsets together, explored new cities together, and built dreams together.

My love for Ravi was one big reason I took so long to write this book, why I continued to procrastinate when my editors would inform me of impending deadlines. Because I could not share my story of growth without sharing my history with Ravi, and there was no way to offer transparency to my readers without casting him in a negative light.

Our love was innocent, it was deep, and it was breathtaking, but it was not meant to carry a lifelong relationship.

There was no capacity for my own personal growth because Ravi was too close to our culture. Too committed to adhering to the expectations of our culture and community. Too keen to accommodate the *log ki kayenge* ("what will people say?") mentality of the South Asian community.

He did the best he could with the tools he'd been given. But his best was not enough for me. My thirst for independence and adamant desire to challenge the customs of our culture intimidated him, and our marriage quickly spiraled downward.

Leaving him was one of the hardest things I've ever done, and even now, years later, I think of him. He still holds a piece of my heart. Love does not disappear when relationships end. It remains an inexorable part of who we are. Even as we evolve and grow, the remnants of who we once were remain with us. So too do the people who loved us and whom we loved in return.

Ravi represents any number of South Asian men in America. He is not a villain, and he is not alone in the beliefs he held.

I will not ask that you show him grace as you process the stories I shared in this book. What I will ask, however, is that you find the Ravis in your own personal life and you share with them what you learned from this book. I ask that you push back on their prejudice, you cast a light on their ignorance, and you offer them opportunities to help create a new narrative within our community. A narrative that accepts, appreciates, and respects people from every community, every culture, and every country, regardless of what they look like, who they love, what God they pray to, or where they come from.

Conclusion

As he was helping me flesh out the content of this book, my developmental editor asked me one afternoon, "Do you think this book redeems you for your past prejudice?"

The question caught me off guard. And it made me think. *Did* I feel that writing this book would somehow make me a better person? Was it self-aggrandizing to think I would create something that people would actually *read* about a subject matter upon which I was still very much a novice myself?

The truth is nothing will redeem me from my past prejudice. On good days, I tell myself I didn't know any better, since I was the by-product of a particular culture that I tore myself away from as soon as I truly realized how much I needed to change. On bad days, I tell myself I was a weak and cowardly person and my inner compass always knew something was off but I was so consumed with the need to be accepted by my family that I ignored what I knew in my gut were red flags.

I don't think any of that matters.

"No," I said to him bluntly. "I think this book will probably make a lot of people look at me differently. It may make them like me less. But that's not the point. The point of the book is to show people you CAN change, you have to work to change, and a lot of the South Asian community's prejudice is based on ignorance and misinformation."

By pulling the curtain back on my own history with prejudice, my hope is people will feel more comfortable reflecting on their own problematic and prejudiced viewpoints.

By sharing that I went from being an active participant and perpetuator of anti-Blackness to building a home and life with a Black man, I hope to show how much joy and happiness is on the other side of becoming a better person.

Being ignorant and myopic isn't a forever state unless you *choose* for it to be. Personal development takes work. Constant work.

And I'm not even remotely close to being as educated as I want to be about race relations in the United States. I'm still learning.

In fact, even the language I use regarding my child's identity is something I am learning to change. In the process of writing my book, I connected with Dr. Jennifer Noble, a licensed psychologist who specializes in educating parents of mixed-race children on how to raise confident, secure mixed-race children.

Dr. Noble's resources have been critical in addressing my anxieties around my child's identity. When we connected over email, she wrote, "If I may offer my own thoughts gently, I'd love for you to consider removing the word 'half' from your descriptions of your baby—using 1/2, 1/4, 'part,' etc. really can do a disservice to how the child understands themselves. Your baby is both Indian AND Black—fully both and a whole person!"

Dr. Noble's words were echoed by Amirah, a mixed South Asian and Black woman based in the UK whom I met over social media.

"One thing that I and a lot of mixed-race people struggle with is what people call us and what we are told to call ourselves," Amirah told me. "Biracial is an odd term for me being from the UK because it's not so common here. I know people have mixed feelings about it though, as well as being called 'half' or a percentage. I guess for a lot of people, we don't really feel like half of anything and feel fully all of ourselves, or at least want to. So for me, I feel South Asian and I feel Black. There's not really a half or a bi- or anything. I'm just fully all of it."

When I shared my concerns over my child's sense of belonging, Amirah was incredibly comforting.

"Your child will grow up and decide the terms they want to use for their own identity," she said. "And that might be language we use now or maybe a new term, who even knows. But to me, your culture and your partner's culture haven't been diluted in you having a child together. They've just kind of joined or merged or formed something new. Less of the either/or, more 'and.'"

For so long, I feared that raising a mixed-raced baby would cause confusion for my child, would lead to the dilution of both my and Mel's respective cultures. Amirah's words filled me with relief.

I share this all to tell you that it's okay if you, like me, are still learning. It's okay if you don't show up perfectly. It's okay to be scared to say the wrong thing. It's okay if your words come out a little messy as you learn to talk about anti-Blackness in our communities.

And I hope you do talk about it because it *is* still an issue.

A few weeks before I submitted the first draft of the manuscript for this book, I dropped my head onto the kitchen table, overwhelmed with insecurity over whether anyone would even read my writing. *Is this book even relevant anymore? It's 2022. Surely things are better now.*

The following week, I went onto my Instagram (which is not set to private) and saw a comment an Indian man had posted on a photograph of me and Mel.

"A golden apple… in the hands of a monkey."

As I marketed the book, I received direct messages on my social media accounts from South Asian men who referred to Mel using racial slurs.

A popular blog called *Growing Up Gupta*, which is run by a Black woman named Nikita Gupta, highlights interracial relationships and spotlights couples who want to share their stories with the community. Nikita, who is married to an Indian man and a mother of two, offered to help me promote my book by writing a feature on me and Mel (which was an honor, as Nikita's blog was the first I came across that ever discussed Black-Indian relationships).

A few days after the blog post went live, someone left nasty comments about Black people, Black children, and my mental sanity for choosing to have a child with a Black man. The person's name was an Indian name.

These experiences, all occurring during the process of revising this book, were an answer to my question. Yes, this book was clearly still relevant.

***

Our baby was born in the early days of January 2022. To our joy and surprise (we were so confident we were having a boy), I gave birth to a beautiful baby girl.

She looks like her father, but she has my large eyes and the shape of my mouth. She has Mel's easygoing temperament and my spunk.

She is stunning. She is happy. She is healthy. She has become, in her short time on Earth, our everything. She is the greatest manifestation of my love for her father. Every day I hold her, I am intentionally grateful for the journey that brought me into Mel's arms and, eventually, her into mine.

Her presence in the world came as a surprise to many in my family. We kept my pregnancy quiet, as it was high-risk. I wanted to be as present as possible in my experience carrying and growing our child.

Once news of her birth spread, the gossip mills began turning almost immediately.

While many people sent my parents words of love and congratulations for being first-time grandparents, certain family members shared their less-than-supportive opinions. That my partner is Black, that I have chosen to not remarry, that I have a baby with a Black man: these facts are all judged.

The gossip about my relationship and baby crossed the oceans to India, where my grandfather ultimately confronted family members who engaged in the negative gossip about his first great-grandchild.

My heart still warms when I think of how happy my grandfather was when he learned of our daughter. We'd been so certain he would react poorly to the news of the baby. I still melt when I see how joyful he is when he holds her, how excited he is when my father sends him videos of our baby.

But my cousins, Punjabi American men and women in their twenties and thirties, have been less than gracious when they heard the news that I have a Black and Indian baby. Even my cousin, who was bullied for getting darker in the sun when we were children, participates in the gossip about my relationship with Mel and my decision to build a family with him.

The reality is older generations can indeed be highly prejudiced and racist, but they can also be surprisingly loving, accepting, and open-minded. Younger generations can be "woke," liberal, and progressive but also small-minded, myopic, and ignorant.

Our community is vast, and opportunities for education and improvement are abundant.

We cannot control others or dictate how they choose to show up in the world, but we can control ourselves and how we choose to show up in this world. We can continue to pursue our best selves, to educate and to advocate so the anti-Blackness we've witnessed or engaged in is no longer considered normal, acceptable, or expected.

And, most importantly, we can all look inward and challenge our own core beliefs to ensure they align with the people we want to be.

And I know that if a woman like me, a woman raised in a conservative Punjabi household, can unlearn decades of conditioning and continue to keep her heart and mind open to learning, then there is hope that our daughter will grow up in a world that is kinder and more accepting than the one experienced by her parents.

I hope this book can help those who need it to tap into their best selves, to untangle themselves from the beliefs, customs, and mores that promote anything other than kindness and equity toward their fellow human beings.

My baby was not just the catalyst for my book. She is now my constant inspiration to be better, to do better. To live a life of love and acceptance, to keep my heart open, and to show my child that at the heart of every person is a human core capable of infinite compassion and love.

Acknowledgments

This book would not be possible without my life partner, Mel. From its inception to its publication, every part of this book was influenced by you, my love. You kissed me and told me I'd be a "prolific writer" so many times, I lost count. Your unshakeable faith in me is my lighthouse. It guides me during my darkest moments and reminds me that with enough grit and perseverance, I can accomplish anything. Thank you for watching our baby so I could write. Thank you for getting up with her all those early mornings so I could rest. Thank you for pushing me to keep writing and revising so I could fulfill my childhood dream of being a published author. Thank you for giving me our daughter: So much of her is you, and I love you both. Words will never adequately express just how much and how deeply.

I want to also thank my parents. Your own stories of growth are the reasons I felt this book could make a difference in the world. You have both challenged yourselves to grow and have astounded me with the depth of your dedication to becoming more accepting and loving people. We've come a long way together, and I'm blessed that you both have walked alongside me as we worked to unlearn the narratives from our culture.

To my cousin, prabh: After losing touch for over a decade and a half, we reconnected because you took the time to talk to me about my dream of writing a book. Our conversation helped me create the framework for this entire project, and your insights helped guide my research.

To my friends Melody, Mira, Julia, Katrina, Lindsay, and Alonya: Each of you played a critical role in supporting me during this eighteen-month journey of pouring my heart and soul into writing my first book. Thank you for being patient with me as I navigated learning how to balance job hunting, new motherhood, and book writing with being a present and attentive friend. I didn't always do a good job of juggling it all, but you never stopped supporting me. You've all shown me the true value of lifelong friendships. I love you all dearly and am blessed every day you choose to love and accept me.

To Shardi: I will always love you and be grateful for the role you played in my life. Till the day I die, you will hold a piece of my heart.

To Nikita: You made time to read my manuscript while juggling being a mama to an active child and a newborn baby. You challenged me to be more vulnerable about my relationship with Mel, and you showed me just how important it was for me to share the message in this book. Thank you.

To Anjuman: I cannot express enough how happy I am our lives connected again. Our phone calls and your feedback helped motivate me to keep working and to keep improving this manuscript. Thank you for making the time for me and showing me yet again what a supportive and selfless friend you are to the people you love.

To Aaron and Key: You both pushed me to share more about Black history and to dig deeper. You gave me confidence in my voice and made me feel like this book was worth writing. I will never be able to say thank you enough.

To Arvinder Auntiji: I know it wasn't easy for you to read this book and hear my thoughts on our culture and community. I am so impressed by how open and receptive you were to my writing and honored that you took the time to share your thoughts with me. Thank you, ji.

To Mark: When we met, I never would have expected you to be such a big part of such a big project in my life. Your encouragement, your time, and your insights were all critical to bringing this book to life. Thank you a million times over, my friend.

To the team at New Degree Press: Thank you for being patient as I figured out how to juggle a newborn baby and a new job with navigating a book publishing journey. And thank you for helping me make my dream of being a published author come true!

And finally, I want to give a special shout-out to every single person who preordered a copy of my book. Each of you breathed life into chapters of my book, and your support kept me motivated to keep writing, to keep revising, and to keep showing up. THANK YOU:

Sherry Lester
Alonya Lowe
Drew Lee
Julia Michelle Anderson
Agnes Poon
Tara Strand
Izzy Leahy
Mel Johnson
Stephanie Bernabe
Cindy Lui
Charles Shumaker
Mira Zurayk
Melody Lavian
Michael Biarnes
Jen Shetland
Rebecca Valdez
Tarryn Rossetti
Kelan Berwick
Anjuman Shah
Lauren Hulit
Ian Chang
May Chen
Yury Adamov
Adam Emery
Gurmeet Sawhney
Pamela Koch
Hanna Alhassen
Katrina Trisko
Nadine Tapia

Pinki Dhillon
Jennifer Gross
Debbie Lin
Zeenat Bhamani
Judy Sherman
Satinderpal Kehal
Kiran Randhawa
Abby Wozniak
Mumtaz Khan
Makenzie Jordan
Monica Lavian
Lauren Mulligan
Michelle Sloan
Navneet Purba
Francisco Peralta
Steven Hammersmark
Steve Urquhart
Elena Kunicki
Lindsay Smith
Jaimee Cooper
Blair Silverman
Cathy Smith
Morgan Bookheimer
Karson Holbrook
Renzo Rossello
Susie Choi
Jamie Hoffman
Rizwana Seeham
Monica Kenney

Beverlee Abell
Tracy Trisko
Melissa Halas
Griffin Danes
Ashley Brown
Sean Clarke
Chris Diaz
Rose Wilson
Kristen Rehnelt
Karen Weiss
Marc Lowe
Diane Mendez
Christine Rosskopf
Ellen Rodriguez
Jessica Janda
Jennifer Cadenhead
Maureen O'Driscoll
Alyssa Bartholomew
Jennifer Sun
Jessica Okui
Eric Koester
Laura Garcia
Ramtin Mobasheri
Ryan Hann
Manish Kumar
Dan Wagstaff
Trish Filamor
Dina D'Alessandro
Michael Garas
Muna Hamideh
Janna Guberman
Patrick Fuhrman

Jon Koegler
Madeline Carpenter
Sharon Bansal
Amanda Callahan
Phil Thibault
Lida Lavian
Sheena Gill
Katharine Rouse
Jessica Gelman
Erika Robles
Nilufer Lakhani
Marissa Hoffman
Patrick Robey
Regina Rangi
Jack Davis
Allen Wagner
Shawnacy Evans-Singh
Sam Cartina
Krysta Cain
Lois Ceglia
Pargat Kehal
John Tindall
Donald Klein
Jay Schoen
Stephanie Gardea
Anca Napau
Susan Tappe
Mijean Ward
Susie Moon
Sunjot Purewal
prabhdeep kehal
Andria Evangel

Courtney Desmarais
Kristi Masser
Tia Mistry
Katy Fraser
Leena Zurayk
LaNita Thompson
Misty Casseus
Michelle Bucell
Walaa Dababneh
Daman Kaur
Diana Rodriguez
Preetika Melville
Aaron Barfield
Jaigurpal Dhillon
Aman Dhaliwal
Yankee Guo
Alyssa Lavy
Eric Addo
Gyorgyi Datz
Pushpinder Pabla
Francisca Pereira
Sana Zurayk
Carrianne Crummett
Sammy Calixto
Simran Basra
Veronica Fortunato
Harleen Kaur
Lovleen Rani
Nikita Gupta
Jillian Rice
Jenna Mills
Claire Haft

Kathy Webb
Raeesa Kerbelker
Marricke Metoyer
Tanya Mitra
Kamilla Rymwid
Anisa Mughal
Jennifer Mesisca
Dugeiby Mateo
Francisco Arias
Ami Patel
Simran Lehal
Summer Groth
Micah Steward
Tripat Chawla
Maneet Gill
Rachana Vaja
Shelby Schermeyer
Albert Saliba
Callie Holloway-Louch
Jasmin Oeztelli
Preston Washington
Kevinn Souffrant
Czarina Mada-Rodríguez
Eric Williams
Rajinder Walcott
Bansi Patel
Jason Machowsky
Arvinder Goomer
Alexia Verdi
Rajvi Vyas
Murali Srivathsa
Kirstine Donato

Bisman Bhatti
Saira Rao
Elizabeth Li
Magali Limeta
Mychael Hamner
Bhavika Panchal
Lauren Marcheskie
Erin Hobson

Nasoan Sheftel-Gomes
Vanessa Lee
Karen Smith
Adrien Hamedi
Karina Salazar
Sharon Hsu
Key Robbins

Appendix

Chapter 1:   Growing Up a Brown Girl in a White World

Basu, Moni. 2016. "15 Years After 9/11, Sikhs Still Victims of Anti-Muslim Hate Crimes." *CNN*. September 15, 2016. https://www.cnn.com/2016/09/15/us/sikh-hate-crime-victims/index.html (accessed October 28, 2022).

Chapter 5:   The Model Minority Myth is a Racial Wedge

Geary, Daniel. 2015. "The Moynihan Report: An Annotated Edition." *The Atlantic*. September 14, 2015. https://www.theatlantic.com/politics/archive/2015/09/the-moynihan-report-an-annotated-edition/404632/ (accessed October 28, 2022).

Lee, Robert G. 2010. "The Cold War Origins of the Model Minority Myth." In *Asian American Studies Now: A Critical Reader*, edited by Jean Yu-Wen Shen Wu, Thomas Chen, and Jean Yu-Wen Shen Wu, 256-271. Ithaca, NY: Rutgers University Press.

Office of Policy Planning and Research. 1965. *The Negro Family: The Case for National Action*. Washington, DC: US Department of Labor.

The Pluralism Project. 2020. "Asians and Asian Exclusion." The Pluralism Project. Harvard University. Accessed October 28, 2022. https://pluralism.org/asians-and-asian-exclusion.

Pew Research Center. 2015. "Modern Immigration Wave Brings 59 Million to US, Driving Population Growth and Change Through 2065: Views of Immigration's Impact on US Society Mixed." Pew Research Center. September 28, 2015. https://www.pewresearch.org/hispanic/2015/09/28/modern-immigration-wave-brings-59-million-to-u-s-driving-population-growth-and-change-through-2065/.

Pettersen, William. 1966. "Success Story, Japanese-American Style." *The New York Times*. January 6, 1966. https://www.nytimes.com/1966/01/09/archives/success-story-japaneseamerican-style-success-story-japaneseamerican.html (accessed October 22, 2022).

US News & World Report. 1966. "Success Story of One Minority Group in the US." *US News & World Report*. December 26, 1966. https://www.dartmouth.edu/~hist32/Hist33/US%20News%20&%20World%20Report.pdf.

Wu, Ellen D. 2015. *Color of Success: Asian Americans and the Origins of the Model Minority*. Princeton, NJ: Princeton University Press.

Wu, Ellen D. 2016. "The Real Reasons the US Became Less Racist Toward Asian Americans." Interviewed by Jeff Guo. *The Washington Post*. November 29, 2016. https://www.washingtonpost.com/news/wonk/wp/2016/11/29/the-real-reason-americans-stopped-spitting-on-asian-americans-and-started-praising-them/ (accessed October 22, 2022).

Chapter 6: The Toll of the Model Minority Myth on Asians

Allard, Mary D. 2011. "Asians in the US Labor Force: Profile of a Diverse Population." *Monthly Labor Review*. Washington, DC: US Bureau of Labor Statistics.

Budiman, Abby, and Neil G. Ruiz. 2021. "Key Facts about Asian Americans, A Diverse and Growing Population." Pew Research Center. April 29, 2021. Accessed October 16, 2022. https://www.pewresearch.org/fact-tank/2021/04/29/key-facts-about-asian-americans/.

Kocchar, Rakesh, and Anthony Cilluffo. 2018. "Income Inequality in the US is Rising Most Rapidly Among Asians." Pew Research Center. July 12, 2018. Accessed October 16, 2022. https://www.pewresearch.org/social-trends/2018/07/12/income-inequality-in-the-u-s-is-rising-most-rapidly-among-asians/.

Lee, Sunmin, Hee-Soon Juon, Genevieve Martinez, Chiehwen E. Hsu, E. Stephanie Robinson, Julie Bawa, and Grace X. Ma. "Model Minority at Risk: Expressed Needs of Mental Health by Asian American Young Adults." *Journal of Community Health* 34, no. 2 (April): 144-52. doi:10.1007/s10900-008-9137-1.

Chapter 7: The U.S. History I Didn't Know

"A Lynching Memorial Unveiled in Duluth." 2003. *The New York Times*. December 5, 2003. https://www.nytimes.com/2003/12/05/opinion/a-lynching-memorial-unveiled-in-duluth.html (accessed October 22, 2022).

Andrews, Evan. 2014. "Was Jim Crow a Real Person?" History.com. January 11, 2022. Accessed October 16, 2022.

https://www.history.com/news/was-jim-crow-a-real-person.

Blakemore, Erin. 2020. "Jim Crow Laws Created 'Slavery by Another Name.'" *National Geographic*. February 5, 2020. https://www.nationalgeographic.com/history/article/jim-crow-laws-created-slavery-another-name (accessed October 16, 2020).

Bridgers, Jeff. 2016. "Signs of Their Times: 'Jim Crow' Was Here." *Picture This* (blog). The Library of Congress. February 18, 2016. https://blogs.loc.gov/picturethis/2016/02/signs-of-their-times-jim-crow-was-here/.

Dray, Philip. 2002. *At the Hands of Persons Unknown: The Lynching of Black America*. New York: Random House.

Equal Justice Initiative. 2017. *Lynching in America: Confronting the Legacy of Racial Terror*. Montgomery, AL: Equal Justice Initiative.

Equal Justice Initiative, 2020. *Reconstruction in America: Racial Violence after the Civil War, 1865-1876*. Montgomery, AL: Equal Justice Initiative.

Flood, Rebecca. 2021. "Furniture Restorer Finds 200-Year-Old Chair Filled with 'Human Hair.'" *Newsweek*. August 24, 2021. https://www.newsweek.com/furniture-restorer-finds-200-year-old-chair-filled-human-hair-slave-1622452 (accessed October 22, 2022).

Held, Amy. 2017. "2nd Noose Found in DC, This Time at African American History Museum." *National Public Radio*. June 1, 2017. https://www.npr.org/sections/thetwo-way/2017/06/01/531034568/noose-found-at-national-museum-of-african-american-history (accessed October 16, 2022).

Ross, Kihana M. 2020. "Call It What It Is: Anti-Blackness." *The New York Times*. June 4, 2020. https://www.nytimes.com/2020/06/04/opinion/george-floyd-anti-blackness.html (accessed October 16, 2022).

Smithsonian National Museum of American History. 2004. *Separate is Not Equal*. Smithsonian National Museum of American History. Accessed October 22, 2022. https://americanhistory.si.edu/brown/history/1-segregated/detail/jim-crow-laws.html.

Waldman, Katy. 2015. "Slave or Enslaved Person?" *Slate*. May 19, 2015. https://slate.com/human-interest/2015/05/historians-debate-whether-to-use-the-term-slave-or-enslaved-person.html (accessed October 16, 2022).

Wills, Matthew. 2020. "Were George Washington's Teeth Taken from Enslaved People?" *JSTOR Daily* (blog). JSTOR. February 25, 2020. https://daily.jstor.org/were-george-washingtons-teeth-taken-from-enslaved-people/.

Chapter 8: The Facts of Today I Didn't Know

Bacher-Hicks, Andrew, Stephen B. Billings, and David J. Deming. 2019. "The School to Prison Pipeline: Long-Run Impacts of School Suspensions on Adult Crime." *National Bureau of Economic Research* 26257 (September). doi:10.3386/w26257.

Badolato, Gia M., Meleah D. Boyle, Robert McCarter, April M. Zeoli, William Terrill, and Monika K. Goyal. 2020. "Racial and Ethnic Disparities in Firearm-Related Pediatric Deaths Related to Legal Intervention." *Pediatrics* 146, no. 6 (December). https://doi.org/10.1542/peds.2020-015917.

Bertrand, Marianne. 2016. "This Problem Has a Name: Discrimination." *Chicago Booth Review* (blog). University of Chicago. May 21, 2016. https://www.chicagobooth.edu/review/problem-has-name-discrimination.

Butler, Kelsey. 2020. "Bias Against Black Women's Hair May Hurt Job Hunt, Study Finds." *Daily Labor Report* (blog). Bloomberg Law. August 12, 2020. https://news.bloomberglaw.com/daily-labor-report/black-womens-natural-hair-may-hinder-job-prospects-study-finds.

Camera, Lauren. 2021. "Study Confirms School-to-Prison Pipeline." *US News & World Report*. July 27, 2021. https://www.usnews.com/news/education-news/articles/2021-07-27/study-confirms-school-to-prison-pipeline (accessed October 16, 2022).

Clayton-Scott, Judith, and Jing Li. 2016. *Black-White Disparity in Student Loan Debt More Than Triples After Graduation*. Washington, DC: The Brookings Institution.

Coleman-Jensen, Alisha, Matthew P. Rabbitt, Christian A. Gregory, and Anita Singh. 2022. *Household Food Security in the United States*. Washington, DC: US Department of Agriculture.

Duffin, Erin. 2022. "US Home Ownership Rate 2021, By Race." 2022. Statista. September 30, 2022. Accessed October 28, 2022. https://www.statista.com/statistics/639685/us-home-ownership-rate-by-race/.

Ely, Danielle M., and Anne K. Driscoll. 2020. "Infant Mortality Statistics in the United States, 2018: Data from the Period Linked Birth/Infant Death." *National Vital Statistics Reports* 69, no. 7 (July): 7-16. https://www.cdc.gov/nchs/data/nvsr/nvsr69/NVSR-69-7-508.pdf.

Gilmore, Amir A., and Pamela J. Bettis. 2021. "Antiblackness and the Adultification of Black Children in a US Prison Nation." *Oxford Research Encyclopedia of Education*. March 25, 2021. https://doi.org/10.1093/acrefore/9780190264093.013.1293.

Goff, Phillip Atiba, Matthew Christian Jackson, Brook Allison Lewis Di Leone, Carmen Marie Culotta, and Natalie Ann DiTomasso. 2014. "The Essence of Innocence: Consequences of Dehumanizing Black Children." *Journal of Personality and Social Psychology* 106, no. 4 (February): 526-45. doi:10.1037/a0035663/.

Gross, Terry. 2017. "A 'Forgotten History' of How the US Government Segregated America." *National Public Radio*. May 3, 2017.

https://www.npr.org/2017/05/03/526655831/a-forgotten-history-of-how-the-u-s-government-segregated-america (accessed October 28, 2022).

Mitchell, Bruce. 2018. "HOLC 'Redlining' Maps: The Persistent Structure of Segregation and Economic Inequality." National Community Reinvestment Coalition. March 20, 2018. Accessed October 28, 2022. https://ncrc.org/holc/.

Koval, Christy Zhou, and Ashleigh Shelby Rosette. 2020. "The Natural Hair Bias in Job Recruitment." *Social Psychological and Personality Science* 12, no. 5 (August): 741-50. https://doi.org/10.1177/1948550620937937.

National Fair Housing Alliance. 2022. "Groundbreaking Report Identifies Bias and Systemic Barriers in Real Estate Appraisals." Accessed October 16, 2022. https://nationalfairhousing.org/groundbreaking-report-identifies-bias-and-systemic-barriers-in-real-estate-appraisals/.

National Institute of Justice. "Student Suspensions Have Negative Consequences, According to NYC Study." National Institute of Justice. November 12, 2021. https://nij.ojp.gov/topics/articles/student-suspensions-have-negative-consequences-according-nyc-study.

Nellis, Ashley. 2021. "The Color of Justice: Racial and Ethnic Disparity in State Prisons." Washington, DC: The Sentencing Project.

Centers for Disease Control and Prevention. 2019. "Racial and Ethnic Disparities Continue in Pregnancy-Related Deaths." *CDC Newsroom.* Accessed October 22, 2022. https://www.cdc.gov/media/releases/2019/p0905-racial-ethnic-disparities-pregnancy-deaths.html.

Social Science Research Solutions (distributor; accessed October 3, 2022). https://doi.org/10.3886/ICPSR38387.v1.

Solis, Gustavo. 2021. "For Black Parents, 'The Talk' Binds Generations and Reflects Changes in America." *USC News* (blog). The

University of Southern California. March 10, 2021. https://news.usc.edu/183102/the-talk-usc-black-parents-children-racism-america/.

US Department of Education Office for Civil Rights. 2014. *Civil Rights Data Collection: Data Snapshot (School Discipline)*. Washington, DC: US Department of Education Office for Civil Rights.

Chapter 10: Colorism in South Asian Culture

Box Office India. 2018. "Top Hits 2019." Box Office India. Accessed October 22, 2022. https://www.boxofficeindia.com/hit-down.php?txtYearlyData=2010-2019&year=2019.

Johari, Aarefa. 2015. "'Skin' Is Not In: Small Victory for Student-Activist in Renaming of 'Skin'-Coloured Crayons." Scroll.in. April 21, 2015. https://scroll.in/article/721970/skin-is-not-in-small-victory-for-student-activist-in-renaming-of-skin-coloured-crayons.

Mahtani, Melissa. 2020. "An Asian Dating Website Has Removed an Option That Asked Users to Specify Their Skin Tone." *CNN*. June 24, 2020. https://www.cnn.com/2020/06/24/us/shaadi-com-removes-skin-tone-filter-trnd/ (accessed October 18, 2022).

McEvoy, Jemina. 2020. "Critics Slam Unilever Rebrand of 'Fair & Lovely' Skin Lightener as 'Glow & Lovely.'" *Forbes*. July 2, 2020. https://www.forbes.com/sites/jemimamcevoy/2020/07/02/critics-slam-unilever-rebrand-of-fair--lovely-skin-lightener-as-glow--lovely/ (accessed October 28, 2022).

Schild, Darcy. 2020. "Johnson & Johnson Will No Longer Sell Skin-Lightening Products Sold Mainly in India, Middle East, and Other Parts of Asia." *Insider*. June 20, 2022. https://www.insider.com/skin-lightening-products-discontinued-neutrogena-clean-and-clear-2020-6 (accessed October 28, 2022).

StrategyR. 2022. "Skin Lighteners: World Market Report." Global Industry Analysts, Inc. https://www.strategyr.com/market-report-skin-lighteners-forecasts-global-industry-analysts-inc.asp.

Srivastava, Roli. 2020. "Beyoncé Reference Cut from Bollywood Song After Racist Lyrics Storm." *Reuters*. September 15, 2020. https://www.reuters.com/article/india-film-bollywood-racism-idUKL8N2GC31F (accessed October 18, 2022).

Vyas, Hetal. 2014. "Teen Files Case Against 'Racially Offensive' Crayon." *Bangalore Mirror*. January 15, 2014. https://bangaloremirror.indiatimes.com/bangalore/crime/hindustan-pencils-crayon-racist-racially-case/articleshow/28796721.cms (accessed October 28, 2022).

Chapter 11: The Impact of Casteism & Colonialism on Anti-Blackness

Bhangle, Devanshi. 2020. "Facing India's Legacy of Colourism." *The McGill International Review*. March 21, 2020. https://www.mironline.ca/facing-indias-legacy-of-colourism/.

Biswas, Soutik. 2020. "Hathras Case: Dalit Women Are among the Most Oppressed in the World." *BBC*. October 6, 2020. https://www.bbc.com/news/world-asia-india-54418513.

Equality Labs. 2018. *Caste in the United States*. USA: Equality Labs.

Human Rights Watch. 2018. "India: Events of 2018." Human Rights Watch. October 22, 2022. https://www.hrw.org/world-report/2019/country-chapters/india.

Iyengar, Rishi. 2020. "California Sues Cisco for Alleged Discrimination Against Employee Because of Caste." *CNN*. July 1, 2020. https://www.cnn.com/2020/07/01/tech/cisco-lawsuit-caste-discrimination/index.html (accessed October 18, 2022).

Kaul, Chandrika. 2011. "From Empire to Independence: The British Raj in India 1858-1947." *History* (blog). BBC.co.uk. March 3, 2011. Accessed October 18, 2022. https://www.bbc.co.uk/history/british/modern/independence1947_01.shtml.

Moreno, Edward J., and Paige Smith. 2022. "Rare Caste Bias Case Advances, Raising Calls for Federal Action." *Daily Labor Report* (blog). Bloomberg Law. August 10, 2022. https://news.bloomberglaw.com/daily-labor-report/rare-caste-bias-case-advances-raising-calls-for-federal-action.

Chapter 12: The Media's Influence on Immigrants

Rodgers, Nicole, and Rashad Robinson. 2017. "How the News Media Distorts Black Families." *The Washington Post*. December 29, 2017. https://www.washingtonpost.com/outlook/2017/12/29/a374a268-ea6d-11e7-8a6a-80acf0774e64_story.html (accessed October 18, 2022).

Staples, Brent. 2021. "How the White Press Wrote Off Black America." *The New York Times*. July 10, 2021. https://www.nytimes.com/2021/07/10/opinion/sunday/white-newspapers-african-americans.html (accessed October 18, 2022).

Chapter 13: "Your Baby Won't Be Black"

"FBI Reports Hate Crimes at Highest Level in 12 Years." 2021. Equal Justice Initiative. September 9, 2021. Accessed October 18, 2022. https://eji.org/news/fbi-reports-hate-crimes-at-highest-level-in-12-years/.

Morrison, Aaron. 2022. "Buffalo Mass Shooting Opens Longstanding Wounds of Black Trauma and Neglect." *PBS News Hour*.

May 22, 2022. https://www.pbs.org/newshour/nation/buffalo-mass-shooting-opens-longstanding-wounds-of-black-trauma-and-neglect (accessed October 18, 2022).

Philimon, Wenei. 2020. "Black Americans Report Hate Crimes, Violence in the Wake of George Floyd Protests and Black Lives Matter Gains." *USA Today*. July 7, 2020. https://www.usatoday.com/story/news/nation/2020/07/07/black-americans-report-hate-crimes-amid-black-lives-matter-gains/3259241001/ (accessed October 22, 2022).

Riddle, Katia. 2022. "Biden Calls for Resignation of LA City Council Members Over Racist Remarks." *National Public Radio*. October 11, 2022. https://www.npr.org/2022/10/11/1128287297/nury-martinez-biden-resignation-la-city-council-racist-remarks (accessed October 18, 2022).

Vera, Amir, and Melissa Alonso. 2021. "Indianapolis Police Sergeant under Federal Investigation after Body Camera Video Showed Him Kicking a Handcuffed Man in the Head." *CNN*. October 13, 2021. https://www.cnn.com/2021/10/12/us/indianapolis-sergeant-charge-head-kick/index.html (accessed October 18, 2022).

Webster, Richard A. 2021. "Three Children Attacked a Black Woman. A Sheriff's Deputy Arrived—and Beat Her More." *ProPublica*. October 16, 2021. https://www.propublica.org/article/three-children-attacked-a-black-woman-a-sheriffs-deputy-arrived-and-beat-her-more (accessed October 18, 2022).

Additional Resources

Adeni, Samra. 2014. "The Empire Strikes Back: Postcolonialism and Colorism in Indian Women." Thesis. Stanford University.

Cooley, Aaron. 2022. "War on Poverty." *Encyclopedia Britannica*. Accessed October 16, 2022. https://www.britannica.com/topic/War-on-Poverty.

Lee, Jin Hee. 2018. "A Lawsuit Seeks to Erase Harvard Applicants' Racial Identity. It Reveals What Some Americans Still Don't Get About Discrimination." *TIME*. August 2018. https://time.com/5370441/harvard-admissions-case-diversity-asian-americans/ (accessed October 22, 2022).

Prashad, Vijay. 2001. *The Karma of Brown Folk*. Minneapolis, MN: University of Minnesota Press.

The Southeast Asia Resource Action Center (SEARAC). 2020. *Southeast Asia American Journeys: A National Snapshot of Our Communities*. Los Angeles, CA: Asian Americans Advancing Justice.

www.ingramcontent.com/pod-product-compliance
Lightning Source LLC
LaVergne TN
LVHW012017060526
838201LV00061B/4340